W9-BEN-923

Fourth Grade Skills

A Best Value Book™

Written by
Patricia Pedigo and Dr. Roger DeSanti

Edited by
Kelley and Aaron Levy

© Carson-Dellosa CD-3761

ISBN 0-88724-546-3

Table of Contents

Word Skills

Math Skills

Fourth Grade Skills

Written by Patricia Pedigo and Dr. Roger DeSanti
Edited by Kelley and Aaron Levy

About the Authors

Patricia Pedigo has many years of teaching experience in urban, rural, public, and private settings. She has taught at all elementary and middle school grade levels, and worked as a reading specialist for learning different students. Patricia has created materials that integrate content areas with language development skills. She holds a M.Ed. in Reading Education and is nearing completion of her doctoral studies.

Dr. Roger DeSanti has been an educator since the mid-1970s. His teaching experiences span a wide range of grades and ability levels, from deaf nurseries through university graduate schools. As a professor, he has authored numerous articles and books, achievement tests, and instructional materials.

Perfect for school or home, every **Kelley Wingate Best Value Book™** has been designed to help students master the skills necessary to succeed. Each book is packed with reproducible test pages, 96 cut-apart flash cards, and supplemental resource pages full of valuable information, ideas, and activities. These activities may be used as classroom or homework activities, or as enrichment material.

This book was developed to provide skills practice in the areas of Reading, Grammar, and Mathematics. Each skill is identified and presented in a range of grade-appropriate ability levels. These activities have been sequenced to facilitate successful completion of the assigned tasks, thus building the self-confidence students need to meet academic challenges.

Ready-to-Use Ideas and Activities

Included in the back of this book are 48 vocabulary and 48 math flash cards ideal for individual review, group solving sessions, or as part of timed, sequential, or grouped activities. Pull out the flash card pages and cut the cards apart with scissors or a paper cutter. Here are just a few of the ways you may want to use these flash cards:

Vocabulary Flash Cards

Bingo Reproduce the Bingo sheet (page iii) for every student. Write the vocabulary flash card words on a chart or chalkboard. Have students choose 24 words and write one in each block of their bingo cards. Cut out the vocabulary flash cards and make them into a deck. Rather than calling out the word itself, call out a definition, antonym, or synonym for the word. Place the called-out words in a separate stack. Students who have the word being described written on their bingo cards should make an "X" through the word. The first student who crosses out five words in a row (horizontally, vertically, or diagonally) wins the game. Check his bingo card against the stack of called-out words. To extend the game, continue playing until students have crossed out all the words on their Bingo cards.

Clue A group of 4 students (teams of 2) can use the vocabulary cards to play "clue." Have children place the cards face down in the middle of a table. The first player selects a card and then gives a one-word clue that describes that word to his partner. If his partner cannot guess the word being suggested, the selected card is given to a member of the opposing team who attempts to get his partner to guess the word. Teams take turns guessing until someone can name the word on the card. The first team to name the word wins a point.

Writing Students can choose cards at random and write a sentence with each word, or write paragraphs or short stories using several of the flash card words.

Vocabulary Write sentences on the board using the vocabulary words but leave blanks in place of the vocabulary words. Have small groups of students take turns sorting through the flash cards to find words that could accurately complete the sentences.

Math Flash Cards

Timed Exercises Use a timer or stopwatch to record how many problems a student can answer correctly in a certain amount of time. Review incorrect answers and repeat the exercise. Provide rewards for improved scores.

Quizzes Use flash cards as impromptu quizzes. Give each student three to five cards attached to an answer sheet that he can complete and return. Vary the selection of cards given to each student for each quiz.

Bonus Questions Post a certain number of cards as bonus questions or for extra credit.

B	I	N	G	O
		FREE		

Rule

A **contraction** is two words joined together with one or more letters omitted and replaced by an apostrophe (').

I would = I'd

was not = wasn't

Rewrite each sentence, changing the underlined words to a contraction.

1. <u>I am</u> going to the movies this Friday.

   _____

2. <u>You are</u> going to be late for school.

   _____

3. <u>He is</u> my best friend.

   _____

4. <u>She would</u> like some ice cream.

   _____

5. <u>They are</u> going to the beach.

   _____

6. The twins <u>are not</u> identical.

   _____

7. The boys <u>were not</u> eating breakfast.

   _____

8. We <u>did not</u> check the answers.

   _____

9. <u>We are</u> having a party today.

   _____

10. <u>Let us</u> begin the lesson.

    _____

11. <u>You have</u> given me plenty of reasons to study.

    _____

12. Joe <u>should not</u> touch the wet paint.

    _____

> **Rule**
> A **contraction** is two words joined together with one or more letters omitted and replaced by an apostrophe (').
>
> I would = I'd
> was not = wasn't

Rewrite each sentence, changing the underlined words to a contraction.

1. She <u>will not</u> run in the race today.

_____

2. <u>They will</u> try again tomorrow.

_____

3. The dogs <u>are not</u> barking.

_____

4. I <u>would not</u> jump in the pool.

_____

5. The class <u>has not</u> gone to lunch.

_____

6. I <u>did not</u> think of that!

_____

7. My television <u>is not</u> working.

_____

8. <u>We have</u> talked about this long enough.

_____

9. <u>They will</u> sing in the chorus.

_____

10. <u>We are</u> happy to meet you.

_____

11. <u>Who is</u> your best friend?

_____

12. <u>Here is</u> a map of the town.

_____

Rule

A **contraction** is two words joined together with one or more letters omitted and replaced by an apostrophe (').

I would = I'd

was not = wasn't

Rewrite each sentence, changing the underlined words to a contraction.

1. <u>They are</u> looking for you now.

   _____

2. <u>Who would</u> believe that story?

   _____

3. <u>I will</u> be home by seven.

   _____

4. <u>They had</u> better obey the rules!

   _____

5. I think <u>she will</u> like your artwork.

   _____

6. I <u>can not</u> come to your party.

   _____

7. Jody <u>did not</u> know what was happening.

   _____

8. Later, <u>you will</u> clean your room.

   _____

9. I <u>did not</u> finish reading that book.

   _____

10. <u>I would</u> like to have pasta for dinner.

   _____

11. Benny <u>does not</u> look happy.

   _____

12. <u>They have</u> landed on the island.

   _____

> **Rule**
> **Its** is a possessive pronoun. **It's** is a contraction for *it is* or *it has*.
> **Your** is a possessive pronoun. **You're** is a contraction for *you are*.
>   *It's a good idea to bring **your** coat. **You're** going to need **its** warmth.*

Complete each sentence with the proper form of *its* or *it's*.

1. The puppy chased _____ tail.

2. _____ a good day for a long walk.

3. We have been waiting and _____ taking too long.

4. The table wobbles because _____ leg is broken.

5. _____ the first time I have seen that.

6. The dog buried _____ bone.

Complete each sentence with the proper form of *your* or *you're*.

1. Is that _____drawing?

2. _____a fine painter.

3. Where will you hang _____ picture?

4. I think _____ nice.

5. _____ mother is calling you.

6. _____ the only one here.

Write four sentences using *its*, *it's*, *your*, and *you're*.

1. _____

2. _____

3. _____

4. _____

Rule

Was and **were** are forms of the verb *be*. Use *was* after a singular subject or after the pronoun *I, he, she,* or *it*. Use *were* after a plural subject or after the pronoun *we, you,* or *they*.
*He **was** glad they **were** coming to the game.*

Complete each sentence with the proper form of *was* or *were*.

1. We _____ just about to leave.

2. Harrison and Mike _____ playing cards.

3. Kelsey _____ jumping rope.

4. The children _____ in the yard.

5. I _____ supposed to call you last night.

6. Marge _____ entering the contest.

7. Joe and Frank _____ playing in the rain.

8. They _____ jumping in the pile of leaves.

9. Cindy _____ baking some oatmeal cookies.

10. The raccoons _____ hiding in the bushes.

11. Jessie and Matt _____ looking for you.

12. The man _____ taking a nap.

Write four sentences using *was* and *were*.

1. _____

2. _____

3. _____

4. _____

Rule

Good is an adjective; it describes a noun. **Well** is an adverb; it describes a verb.
You can also use *well* as an adjective to mean "healthy."

It's a *good* idea to study.   You scored *well* on the test.   He is a *well* man now.
adjective   *adverb*   *adjective (healthy)*

Complete each sentence with the proper form of *good* or *well*.

1. You sang _____ in the concert.

2. It was a _____ day for a hike.

3. I was ill, but now I feel _____ .

4. The floor is a _____ place to play with jacks.

5. He is a _____ looking man.

6. That meat was roasted _____ !

7. My puppy is _____ now, although he had been quite ill.

8. James always comes up with _____ ideas.

9. Casey is a _____ soccer player.

10. Our team will play _____ in the game.

11. The doctor gave him medicine to make him _____.

12. That is a very _____ pie!

Write four sentences using *good* and *well*.

1. _____

2. _____

3. _____

4. _____

Rule
Different words that have almost the same meaning are called **synonyms**.
Beautiful and *lovely* are synonyms.

Read the sentences and choices below. Circle the word that means almost the same thing as the word that is underlined in the sentence.

1. Patsy is <u>active</u> in the drama club. She acts and paints scenery.

   ability   **busy**   **hard**

2. The <u>youngster</u> wandered away from her mother.

   stubby   **subject**   **child**

3. Jerry gave lots of <u>affection</u> to his dog because they were best friends.

   love   **blankets**   **unusual**

4. The flower in the vase began to <u>wither</u> and turn brown.

   dry   **grow**   **speck**

5. Please do not <u>annoy</u> Chris. He has lots of homework to do.

   excuse   **bother**   **ignore**

6. Jonathan <u>placed</u> the books on the shelf.

   removed   **lined**   **put**

7. The <u>antique</u> book was dated 1866.

   modern   **musty**   **old**

8. The word the teacher used was <u>unfamiliar</u> to me.

   unknown   **easy**   **collected**

9. Mary wanted to get an "A" on the test, but she was <u>content</u> with a "B."

   admit   **satisfied**   **upset**

10. Justine knew that if she worked hard she would <u>achieve</u> success.

    attract   **reach**   **struggle**

Rule

Different words that have almost the same meaning are called **synonyms**.
Beautiful and *lovely* are synonyms.

Read the sentences and choices below. Circle the word that means almost the same thing as the word that is underlined in the sentence.

1. It you <u>connect</u> the dots, they will make a picture!

   erase   **draw**   **join**

2. If you <u>intend</u> to finish painting before dinner, you had better hurry.

   plan   **involve**   **dodge**

3. I don't care for spinach. In fact, I <u>detest</u> it.

   enjoy   **hate**   **humble**

4. Can you <u>identify</u> the continents of the world?

   travel   **color**   **name**

5. Do you like my new shoes? Please give me your <u>honest</u> opinion.

   truthful   **fringe**   **desired**

6. The bird's nest was hidden in the <u>shrubs</u> outside the window.

   shuffles   **dark**   **bushes**

7. My mind is made up, so it will do no good to <u>quarrel</u> with me.

   argue   **neglect**   **sniffle**

8. Harvey shoveled a <u>mound</u> of snow off the sidewalk.

   pile   **dribble**   **sod**

9. The letter is so <u>skinny</u>, I can slide it right under the door.

   fat   **thin**   **heavy**

10. The soldier marched <u>onward</u> all day and night.

    quivering   **loudly**   **ahead**

> **Rule**
> Different words that have almost the same meaning are called **synonyms**.
> *Beautiful* and *lovely* are synonyms.

Read the sentences and choices below. Circle the word that means almost the same thing as the word that is underlined in the sentence.

1. Your mother said to call her right now. She said it is <u>urgent</u>!

   silly   **willow**   **important**

2. I want to sit near the window. Will you <u>switch</u> seats with me?

   swarm   **trade**   **build**

3. There was not one <u>speck</u> of dirt anywhere when Mom finished cleaning!

   spike   **bucket**   **spot**

4. It took me an hour, but I finally found the <u>solution</u> to that problem.

   answer   **number**   **prime**

5. The children picked up all the <u>litter</u> and threw it in the garbage can.

   shrimp   **trash**   **extra**

6. Delaney was <u>confident</u> she knew the answer to the question.

   certain   **unsure**   **happy**

7. It is not healthy to <u>expose</u> your skin to the hot sun for so long.

   bare   **soften**   **cover**

8. Students will <u>display</u> their projects in the art room next week.

   glimpse   **show**   **feast**

9. The house looked <u>eerie</u> sitting on top of the hill in those shadows.

   strange   **bright**   **lower**

10. The hikers began to <u>ascend</u> the mountain.

    climb   **raise**   **draw**

Rule

Different words that have almost the same meaning are called **synonyms**.
Beautiful and *lovely* are synonyms.

Read the sentences and choices below. Circle the word that means almost the same thing as the word that is underlined in the sentence.

1. I have a <u>job</u> to do for my dad before I can play.

   chore   **illness**   **lunch**

2. We must <u>alert</u> the town that the flood is coming this way!

   drive   **buckle**   **warn**

3. Yolanda hurt her <u>backbone</u> when she fell off the horse.

   spine   **ankle**   **shoulder**

4. I have pushed for five minutes, but I can't <u>budge</u> this heavy box!

   open   **paint**   **move**

5. Larry <u>challenged</u> me to a race across the yard.

   spoiled   **dared**   **hinted**

6. The store was <u>destroyed</u> in the fire.

   ruined   **built**   **festive**

7. Melanie was <u>furious</u> when Pete insulted her.

   shy   **angry**   **happy**

8. The <u>joyous</u> sound of bells made me smile.

   sad   **happy**   **golden**

9. Jan got a <u>nasty</u> cut on her knee from the sharp rocks.

   bad   **soft**   **cute**

10. The hat looks <u>ridiculous</u> on my brother, so I made him remove it.

    fine   **silly**   **great**

Name _____   Skill: Antonyms

Rule
Words that have opposite meanings are called **antonyms**. *Before* and *after* are antonyms.

Read the sentences and choices below. Circle the word that means the opposite of the word that is underlined in the sentence.

1. That <u>bald</u> baby has a shiny head.

   quiet   **hairy**   **smiling**

2. I don't play the piano well because I am just a <u>beginner</u>.

   child   **expert**   **player**

3. The party has just <u>begun</u>!

   arose   **started**   **ended**

4. The tea tasted <u>bitter</u>, so Macey made a face when she swallowed it.

   nasty   **sweet**   **sour**

5. The <u>bold</u> warrior marched fearlessly into battle.

   timid   **brave**   **old**

6. Sukie <u>cautiously</u> crossed the busy street.

   slowly   **simply**   **recklessly**

7. The <u>cloudless</u> sky was a brilliant blue today.

   cloudy   **plain**   **beautiful**

8. Ned will <u>combine</u> the sand and soil in one large bucket.

   dig   **separate**   **lower**

9. Jessie will <u>complete</u> her project by the end of the week.

   finish   **start**   **fix**

10. The man <u>confessed</u> that he was afraid of many things.

   admitted   **sampled**   **denied**

© Carson-Dellosa CD-3761   11

Rule

Words that have opposite meanings are called **antonyms**.

Before and *after* are antonyms.

Read the sentences and choices below. Circle the word that means the opposite of the word that is underlined in the sentence.

1. We could hear the <u>constant</u> dripping of the faucet all night.

    irregular   **unending**   **angry**

2. Ice will <u>thaw</u> in the warmer weather.

    freeze   **drip**   **melt**

3. Dad had to <u>crouch</u> to see into the little doghouse.

    stand   **crawl**   **squint**

4. The woman proved she was <u>innocent</u>. She had not stolen the watch.

    honest   **home**   **guilty**

5. That was an <u>excellent</u> movie and I enjoyed it!

    terrible   **wonderful**   **short**

6. I will <u>lend</u> you a pencil so you can finish your homework.

    five   **borrow**   **sharpen**

7. The fire <u>destroyed</u> everything in its path.

    ruined   **burned**   **created**

8. The artist was <u>modest</u> about the many awards he had been given.

    boastful   **shy**   **quiet**

9. The mother was <u>frantic</u> when she lost her child in the crowd.

    helpful   **calm**   **upset**

10. Put a little water on this cloth so that it will be <u>moist</u>.

    damp   **wet**   **dry**

Rule
Words that have opposite meanings are called **antonyms**.
Before and *after* are antonyms.

Read the sentences and choices below. Circle the word that means the opposite of the word that is underlined in the sentence.

1. We <u>rarely</u> go outside in this freezing weather.

     seldom   **never**   **often**

2. The hot, dry air was <u>cruel</u> to our skin!

     smart   **mean**   **kind**

3. Mr. Greene was <u>furious</u> when the dog dug up his flowers.

     delighted   **angry**   **wild**

4. The airplane began to <u>descend</u> from the sky toward the runway.

     sway   **rise**   **dip**

5. You were <u>fortunate</u> to find your ring after you lost it in the sand!

     lucky   **unlucky**   **smart**

6. The coach will <u>divide</u> the group into four teams.

     call   **separate**   **unite**

7. I get a lot of <u>pleasure</u> from reading good books.

     fun   **pain**   **work**

8. That roasted turkey looks <u>plump</u> and juicy!

     fat   **golden**   **slender**

9. The hungry boy <u>devoured</u> his dinner in less than a minute!

     cooked   **nibbled**   **watched**

10. There are <u>countless</u> stars in the night sky!

     amount   **few**   **shiny**

Rule

Words that have opposite meanings are called **antonyms**.

Before and *after* are antonyms.

Read the sentences and choices below. Circle the word that means the opposite of the word that is underlined in the sentence.

1. On the whole team, John can throw the ball the <u>farthest</u>.

   fastest   **nearest**   **best**

2. Julia <u>hastily</u> hid the note under her book as the teacher walked by.

   slowly   **angrily**   **quickly**

3. Keaton <u>crumpled</u> up the paper and threw it away.

   picked   **wrinkled**   **smoothed**

4. The <u>raw</u> meat was not ready to be eaten.

   cooked   **red**   **bitter**

5. The <u>eldest</u> child was a girl and the rest were boys.

   prettiest   **first**   **youngest**

6. Tessie was full of <u>grief</u> when she lost her pet rabbit.

   happiness   **sadness**   **sleepy**

7. The cowboys <u>captured</u> the wild horses in the canyon.

   trapped   **caught**   **released**

8. The <u>entrance</u> to the school was near the gym.

   exit   **door**   **fountain**

9. It was so <u>foggy</u>, I could barely see to drive down the road.

   dark   **misty**   **clear**

10. At what time does the plane for Boston <u>depart</u>?

   arrive   **leave**   **fly**

Rule

Words that are pronounced the same way but have different meanings and spellings are called **homophones**.

Flower and *flour* are homophones.

Read the sentences and choices below. For each sentence, write the correct word in the blank.

1. If _____ ready, we can leave now.

   your   **you're**

2. Drive the tent _____ into the ground.

   stake   **steak**

3. I would like a _____ of pie, please.

   peace   **piece**

4. Does the puppy have muddy _____?

   pause   **paws**

5. Marcus could _____ the radio.

   hear   **here**

6. Did the _____ stop the car in time?

   brakes   **breaks**

7. The school _____ played in the parade.

   band   **banned**

8. I would like to _____ that shirt blue.

   die   **dye**

9. The two boys _____ the boat across the lake.

   road   **rowed**   **rode**

10. What should Pearl _____ to the party?

    ware   **wear**

Name _____   Skill: Homophones

> **Rule**
> Words that are pronounced the same way but have different meanings and spellings are called **homophones**.
> *Flower* and *flour* are homophones.

Read the sentences and choices below. Write the correct word in the blank.

1. Doris likes _____ on her hot dog.

   chilly   chili

2. Jimmy was _____ during the meeting.

   board   bored

3. We must _____ before the storm hits!

   flea   flee

4. Velma got her _____ cut quite short.

   hair   hare

5. What crops were _____ this year?

   grown   groan

6. Joe attached the sun catcher to the _____ in the window.

   pain   pane

7. My favorite dish is _____ and potato soup.

   leak   leek

8. The guide _____ the group to safety.

   lead   led

9. Max took the _____ and guided the horse home.

   rains   reins   reigns

10. The green _____ is a tasty fruit.

    pair   pear   pare

Name _____

Rule

Words that are pronounced the same way but have different meanings and spellings are called **homophones**.

Flower and *flour* are homophones.

Read the sentences and choices below. Write the correct word in the blank.

1. Has the _____ been delivered yet?

   mail   **male**

2. There is _____ way I can do that for you.

   know   **no**

3. Calvin _____ her a dozen roses.

   scent   **sent**

4. Which _____ will we take to Florida?

   route   **root**

5. Those silk flowers look so _____ .

   real   **reel**

6. Mother _____ out the wet clothes.

   wrung   **rung**

7. The flag was hanging on a tall _____ .

   pole   **poll**

8. I do not like to eat the _____ of the egg.

   yoke   **yolk**

9. Sandy's family moved to _____ last year.

   main   **Maine**   **mane**

10. Those shoes gave me a blister on my _____ .

   heal   **heel**   **he'll**

Name _____ Skill: Homophones

> **Rule**
> Words that are pronounced the same way but have different meanings and spellings are called **homophones**.
>
> *Flower* and *flour* are homophones.

Read the sentences and choices below. Write the correct word in the blank.

1. How much does the cat _____ ?

   way   **weigh**

2. I like to _____ the foods I eat each day.

   vary   **very**

3. We watched the _____ leave the beach.

   tied   **tide**

4. Does an elephant have a long _____ ?

   tail   **tale**

5. Martha had to _____ the dogs away.

   shoe   **shoo**

6. The _____ in this play is very long.

   scene   **seen**

7. Jason broke three _____ in the window.

   pains   **panes**

8. Did you _____ at the presents?

   peek   **peak**

9. There are _____ books on the desk.

   for   **fore**   **four**

10. The _____ called for her lamb.

    ewe   **you**

Rule

Words that we understand and use in our daily language are called our **vocabulary**.

Complete each sentence by circling the word that means about the same thing as the underlined word or phrase.

1. A word that means <u>a baby duck</u> is ...
   chick   **duckling**   **egg**

2. To <u>make longer</u> is to ...
   decrease   **supply**   **extend**

3. A <u>mask</u> is a ...
   initial   **disguise**   **lid**

4. The word <u>exhibit</u> means ...
   show   **enter**   **wander**

5. Another word for <u>educate</u> is ...
   apply   **school**   **teach**

6. To <u>exist</u> is to ...
   leave   **live**   **run**

7. When you <u>doze</u> you are ...
   swimming   **writing**   **sleeping**

8. Another word for <u>climate</u> is ...
   weather   **scale**   **land**

9. Another word for <u>sturdy</u> is ...
   rugged   **weak**   **tall**

10. A person who is <u>composed</u> is ...
    calm   **upset**   **tired**

Name _____   Skill: Vocabulary

Complete each sentence by circling the word that means about the same thing as the underlined word or phrase.

1. A word that means <u>to join together</u> is ...
   confuse   **connect**   **blunder**

2. To <u>motion</u> is to ...
   gesture   **vanish**   **explain**

3. A <u>procession</u> is a ...
   nation   **role**   **parade**

4. A word that means <u>sad</u> is ...
   mournful   **plank**   **scarlet**

5. Another word for <u>area</u> is ...
   meter   **outfit**   **region**

6. To <u>find something</u> is to ...
   lighten   **locate**   **marvel**

7. When you <u>move forward</u> you ...
   progress   **fail**   **muffle**

8. Another word for <u>messy</u> is ...
   sloppy   **slippery**   **slant**

9. A <u>suggestion</u> is a ...
   joke   **demand**   **proposal**

10. A person who <u>watches</u> is an ...
   inventor   **observer**   **ostrich**

Rule
Words that we understand and use in our daily language are called our **vocabulary**.

Complete each sentence by circling the word that means about the same thing as the underlined word or phrase.

1. A word that means <u>to pause</u> is ...

    impress   **dare**   **hesitate**

2. To <u>amaze</u> is to ...

    gulp   **dazzle**   **launch**

3. A <u>cloth used at dinner</u> is a ...

    napkin   **plot**   **lodge**

4. A word that means <u>to answer a question</u> is ...

    slither   **contain**   **respond**

5. The word <u>seize</u> means ...

    skim   **process**   **grab**

6. To <u>pollute</u> is to ...

    clean   **dirty**   **bandage**

7. When you feel <u>prickly all over</u> you ...

    tingle   **waddle**   **stitch**

8. Another word for <u>tired</u> is ...

    tread   **weary**   **sturdy**

9. A word that means <u>to change</u> is ...

    chase   **count**   **alter**

10. A person who is <u>part of the family</u> is a ...

    relative   **inspector**   **numeral**

Name _____   Skill: Vocabulary

Rule

Words that we understand and use in our daily language are called our **vocabulary**.

Complete each sentence by circling the word that means about the same thing as the underlined word or phrase..

1. A word that means <u>faithful</u> is ...
   rickety   **honest**   **loyal**

2. To <u>get something back</u> is to ...
   split   **retreat**   **recover**

3. To <u>rest from work</u> is to ...
   outwit   **mingle**   **relax**

4. The word <u>recent</u> means ...
   give   **hate**   **lately**

5. Another word for <u>parcel</u> is ...
   package   **scrub**   **remark**

6. To be <u>modest</u> is to be ...
   humble   **boastful**   **sore**

7. When you <u>embroider</u> you ...
   intend   **sew**   **graze**

8. A word that means <u>huge</u> is ...
   massive   **skinny**   **social**

9. A word that means <u>crimson</u> is ...
   red   **instinct**   **kidnap**

10. To <u>make someone believe</u> is to ...
   border   **cloak**   **convince**

> **Rule**
> When you come to a word you don't know, use **context clues** (the meaning of the rest of the sentence or paragraph) to help you understand its meaning.

Use the context clues to figure out the meaning of each underlined word below. Circle the correct meaning.

1. After losing the lead in the second lap, Michael <u>regained</u> it in the third.

   got back   **finished**

   fell behind   **stumbled**

2. Betsy Ross was a <u>patriot</u>. She made the first flag for the United States.

   an artist   **a traitor**

   a chef   **a person loyal to a country**

3. Gazelle pulled a muscle in her <u>thigh</u> while running in the race.

   part of the hand   **part of the leg**

   part of the shoulder   **a puppet**

4. The artist wore a <u>smock</u> to protect her clothes from the paint.

   curtain   **a long, loose shirt**

   bag   **a rubber band**

5. This paper is due in one hour, so make all <u>haste</u> to get it done!

   erasers   **careful**

   speed   **time**

6. The watch had a <u>luminous</u> face. I could see it in the dark.

   round   **dark**

   lighted   **purple**

7. The police were in <u>pursuit</u> of the man who robbed the bank.

   following   **anger**

   video taping   **running from**

8. I must <u>inform</u> you that you are standing in the wrong line for those tickets.

   ask   **supply**

   tell   **push**

Name _____

Rule

When you come to a word you don't know, use **context clues** (the meaning of the rest of the sentence or paragraph) to help you understand its meaning.

Use the context clues to figure out the meaning of each underlined word below. Circle the correct meaning.

1. Acorns are <u>plentiful</u> in an oak forest.

    unusual   **abundant**

    large   **rare**

2. The lost pilot used the radio to make <u>contact</u> with the control tower.

    touch   **direct**

    communicate   **lean on**

3. My <u>method</u> of making a bed is to pull the cover over everything and walk away!

    way or system   **quilt**

    development   **corner**

4. The vase began to <u>wobble</u> and almost fell, but I caught it in time.

    tip back and forth   **sing**

    turn colors   **shatter**

5. The newspaper was old, yellow, and <u>brittle</u>, so we handled it very carefully.

    green   **easily broken**

    hard   **soft**

6. Mr. Thomas is a stamp <u>collector</u>. He keeps them all in a big album.

    person who eats out   **a customer**

    person who lies   **person who gathers things**

7. Vera shows great <u>affection</u> to her little sister because she loves her.

    fond or tender feelings   **anger**

    happiness   **fear of**

8. The hunters set out several <u>snares</u> to catch the rabbits.

    leashes   **traps**

    branches   **carrots**

Rule
When you come to a word you don't know, use **context clues** (the meaning of the rest of the sentence or paragraph) to help you understand its meaning.

Use the context clues to figure out the meaning of each underlined word below. Circle the correct meaning.

1. The child looked <u>bewildered</u> when she couldn't find her mother in the crowd.

    excited   **confused**

    lazy   **dizzy**

2. Does your purse <u>contain</u> a comb and a wallet?

    hold   **buy**

    use   **unwrap**

3. Jamie seemed very <u>earnest</u> about his plan.

    bashful   **untruthful**

    happy   **serious**

4. Don <u>challenged</u> Marcus to a race around the track.

    invited   **dared**

    threw   **fought**

5. After a good dinner and a warm bath, I feel <u>mellow</u>.

    tense   **upset**

    excited   **relaxed**

6. The hot water made my new shirt <u>shrink</u> and now it doesn't fit me.

    get larger   **discolor**

    get smaller   **fade**

7. I have a <u>request</u> of you. Please wipe your feet before coming in.

    favor to ask   **demand**

    statement   **reply**

8. Rain has been <u>scarce</u> lately, so the ground is dry.

    heavy   **plentiful**

    rare   **messy**

Rule

When you come to a word you don't know, use **context clues** (the meaning of the rest of the sentence or paragraph) to help you understand its meaning.

Use the context clues to figure out the meaning of each underlined word below. Circle the correct meaning.

1. I was very <u>tense</u> before I took that test.

    wonderful   **glad**

    nervous   **angry**

2. She smiled in <u>triumph</u> when she won the race!

    sneer   **victory**

    fear   **jealousy**

3. Dripping water is an <u>annoyance</u> when I am trying to study.

    fun time   **soothing sound**

    experience   **bother**

4. These two paintings are so much alike, I can't tell which is real and which is an <u>imitation</u>!

    copy   **western**

    unusual   **connection**

5. I really like the <u>flavor</u> of that new soda you bought. I drank the whole bottle!

    price   **color**

    advertisement   **taste**

6. I didn't mean to <u>neglect</u> you, but I have been too busy to see you lately.

    ignore   **play with**

    frighten   **share**

7. My shirt <u>shrunk</u> when it was washed in hot water.

    stretched   **froze**

    got smaller   **disappeared**

8. The howling puppies made such a <u>racket</u>, my neighbors called to complain.

    playful   **game**

    noise   **paddle**

Rule
When you come to a word you don't know, use **context clues** (the meaning of the rest of the sentence or paragraph) to help you understand its meaning.

Use the context clues to figure out the meaning of each underlined word below. Circle the correct meaning.

1. The ending of the play was <u>tragic</u>. The main character died.

   too short   **sad or serious**

   a wild, fun time   **beginning**

2. The <u>weary</u> hikers dragged themselves the last three miles of the long walk.

   wiggly   **tired**

   soggy   **mean**

3. The cup held a lot of water because of its large <u>volume</u>.

   handle   **color**

   saucer   **amount of space**

4. Devon looked <u>ridiculous</u> in that baby bunny costume.

   silly   **dramatic**

   respectful   **serious**

5. Those two boys look very <u>similar</u>. Are they twins or just brothers?

   tall   **different**

   alike   **skinny**

6. Have you <u>recovered</u> from that horrible cold?

   sneezing   **gotten better**

   warm   **become worse**

7. Her apology sounded <u>sincere</u>.

   false   **shameful**

   honest   **funny**

8. Nelson wants to be a <u>doctor</u> when he grows up.

   nurse   **actor**

   physician   **man**

Rule
Comprehension questions test your ability to understand what you have read.
When you understand a sentence or story, you **comprehend** it.

Read the story, then answer the questions about it.

Karen curled up on her bed with her favorite book. What a wonderful afternoon this would be! Karen had the house to herself for three hours, while her mom was visiting next door. She planned to eat snacks in her room, finish the book she was reading, and then watch television. As she lay on her bed, she thought about how quiet the house seemed. She could hear the clock ticking in the kitchen at the other end of the house. She could hear children playing outside across the street. Suddenly she heard something that didn't belong in her quiet world. Was someone at the back door? Karen's heart began to race as she heard the door creak open and then close. The next sound she heard was a familiar voice, "Karen, I'm home!"

1. **A good title for this story would be:**
   a. A Good Book
   b. Wasting the Day
   c. Home Alone in the Afternoon
2. **What three things did Karen plan to do that afternoon?**_____

_____

3. **What is a word that means "a harsh, squeaking sound"?**
   a. curled
   b. creak
   c. ticking
4. **Why was Karen home alone?**_____

_____

_____

5. **What words in the story tell you that Karen is scared?**_____

_____

_____

6. **What would you do if you were Karen? Explain why.**_____

_____

Rule

Comprehension questions test your ability to understand what you have read.
When you understand a sentence or story, you **comprehend** it.

Read the story, then answer the questions about it.

Carla pulled herself and her brother's sled up Blackmon's Hill. "What am I doing here?" she thought. "What if I get to the top and have to walk down?" The snowfall the day before had created perfect conditions for sledding. Kids of all ages and even parents were squealing as they went down the hill that leveled out in a wheat field that was now a soft, white blanket. Carla had never sledded anywhere but in the gentle slope of her backyard. What was it like to go so fast? What if she fell? She didn't want to look silly, but she was determined to conquer her fears. Then she saw Natalie sail by. She had baby-sat Natalie last summer! That did it! When Carla arrived at the top, she took a deep breath, pushed off, shut her eyes, and enjoyed the ride!

1. **A good title for this story would be:**
   a. Carla and Natalie
   b. Blackmon's Hill
   c. Carla Conquers Her Fears
2. **Why was Carla determined to sled the hill?**_____

   _____

3. **What is a word that means "conquer"?**
   a. forget
   b. overcome
   c. think about
4. **How does Carla feel about going down the hill?**_____

   _____

   _____

5. **How old do you think Carla and Natalie are?**

   _____

6. **What would you do if you were Carla? Explain.**_____

   _____

   _____

> **Rule**
> **Comprehension** questions test your ability to understand what you have read.
> When you understand a sentence or story, you **comprehend** it.

Read the story, then answer the questions about it.

The plane's tires screeched as they hit the runway. R.J. leaned forward to watch as the passengers began to get off the plane. He had been waiting for this day for so long. His father was in the Navy and had been out on a submarine for a long time. It had been almost a year since R.J. had seen his dad. They wrote letters almost every week, but that wasn't the same as being together. The rush of passengers passed and still his father didn't come. R.J.'s excitement began to turn to disappointment as the last few passengers left the plane. His father wasn't there after all. But wait! What was this huge bear being pushed through the door? Suddenly his father's face peeked over its shoulder. Dad was home at last!

1. **A good title for this story would be:**
    a. The Airport
    b. R.J.'s Day
    c. Dad Comes Home
2. **Why was R.J. at the airport?**_____

    _____

3. **What is a word that means "sadness"?**
    a. disappointment
    b. excitement
    c. peeked
4. **How long had it been since R.J. had seen his dad?**_____

    _____

5. **Why do you think his father was the last person off the plane?**_____

    _____

    _____

6. **Who would you most like to see getting off a plane? Explain why.** _____

    _____

    _____

Rule
Comprehension questions test your ability to understand what you have read.
When you understand a sentence or story, you **comprehend** it.

Read the story, then answer the questions about it.

Mrs. Jamison bent over her work on this warm spring day. She wanted to plant a vegetable garden to surprise her husband. He had not been well all winter, and fresh vegetables were his favorite food. Mr. Jamison had planted a garden every year for the forty-nine years they had been married. This year he was too sick to get outside. Mrs. Jamison was not in the best health herself, but she was determined to plant this garden. She took up the shovel and began the task of turning the soil. Suddenly she heard someone call her name. She looked up and saw ten-year-old David Lawson, her neighbor, standing in her yard with a shovel over his shoulder.

1. **A good title for this story would be:**
   a. Planting Seeds
   b. Gardening is Hard Work
   c. Mrs. Jamison's Garden
2. **What was Mrs. Jamison doing?**_____

   _____

3. **What is a word that means "to make up one's mind"?**
   a. determine
   b. health
   c. poorly
4. **How long had the Jamisons been married?**_____

   _____

5. **What clues in the story let you know the Jamisons are older people?**

   _____

   _____

6. **Why do you think David Lawson has his shovel? Explain.**_____

   _____

   _____

Rule
Comprehension questions test your ability to understand what you have read. When you understand a sentence or story, you **comprehend** it.

Read the story, then answer the questions about it.

Yolanda smiled as she warmed the bottle of milk. Baby-sitting was her favorite thing to do, and this baby was a joy to care for because she was never fussy. Baby-sitting is pretty easy when you like children and Yolanda loved kids. She was very good at her job. Last year she took classes at the hospital that taught her how to care for babies and small children. She learned whom to call in an emergency and how to help a child that is choking. The classes made her more confident that she could handle almost any problem that might arise. She had a lot of fun watching the babies and playing with the children. Best of all, Yolanda was paid good money for a job she loved doing. What a great deal!

1. **A good title for this story would be:**
   a. Yolanda's Job
   b. Baby-sitting is No Fun
   c. Handling Babies
2. **What is Yolanda's job?**_____

_____

3. **What is a word that means "an event that needs action or attention"?**
   a. hospital
   b. baby-sitting
   c. emergency
4. **Why does Yolanda feel so confident?**_____

_____

_____

5. **Why does Yolanda feel so good about her work?**_____

_____

6. **What would you like/not like about baby-sitting? Explain why.**_____

_____

_____

Rule

Comprehension questions test your ability to understand what you have read.
When you understand a sentence or story, you **comprehend** it.

Read the story, then answer the questions about it.

People and animals eat plants. Did you know that some plants eat animals? The sundew plant is covered with tiny hairs and a sticky liquid. The liquid sparkles in the sun and catches the attention of, and then attracts an insect. As soon as the insect lands in the liquid, it becomes stuck. The hairs close over the insect and the plant digests, or eats it! There is another plant that can catch worms. The plant is a tiny fungus that spreads through the ground like thin threads. The threads have little loops growing on them that look like lassos. As a tiny worm crawls through the soil and passes through the loops, the loops tighten and the worm is caught. The fungus then digests the worm.

1. **A good title for this story would be:**
   a. Animals that Eat Plants
   b. Plants that Eat Animals
   c. Why We Live in Communities

2. **What makes insects come to the sundew plant?**_____

   _____

3. **What is a word that means "pull or draw closer"?**
   a. attract
   b. digest
   c. jump

4. **How does the fungus catch worms?**_____

   _____

   _____

5. **What are the loops on the fungus compared to?**_____

   _____

   _____

6. **Which plant would you like to know more about? Why?**_____

   _____

Rule

Comprehension questions test your ability to understand what you have read. When you understand a sentence or story, you **comprehend** it.

Read the story, then answer the questions about it.

A lot of people have gardens in their yards. Gardens that are used to grow food are called *kitchen* or *vegetable gardens*. During World War II, these gardens were also called *victory gardens*. Some people like to grow plants that look pretty in their gardens. Many of these are *flower gardens* because they are filled with irises, roses, tulips, or other plants that flower. Plants that are raised to be researched, studied, or exhibited are kept in *botanical gardens*. Huge gardens that are kept beautiful year-round are often called *formal gardens*. There are gardens for every kind of plant you can think of, including cacti, trees, and pond plants. There are even *rock gardens*! These contain rocks and plants that are well-suited to grow among them.

1. **A good title for this story would be:**
   a. All Types of Gardens
   b. Vegetable Gardens Grow Food
   c. Formal Gardens are Pretty

2. **What did people call vegetable gardens during World War II?** _____

   _____

3. **What is a word that means "to study"?**
   a. botanical
   b. exhibit
   c. research

4. **Which kind of garden might you find at a castle or palace? Why?** _____

   _____

   _____

5. **Which type of garden would you like to have? Why?** _____

   _____

   _____

> **Rule**
> **Comprehension** questions test your ability to understand what you have read. When you understand a sentence or story, you **comprehend** it.

Read the story, then answer the questions about it.

> *The beginning of eternity,*
> *The end of time and space,*
> *The beginning of every end,*
> *The end of every place.*

The words in the box make a riddle. This riddle describes something. Can you guess what it is? It's the letter "E"! Riddles have been used for thousands of years as a way to answer questions. Long ago, not many people could read or had the time to go to school. Knowledge was considered very valuable. When people were given a riddle instead of the answer, it helped them find the answer on their own. If they could not figure out the riddle, they would never know the answer to their question! Today, we use riddles more for fun than for knowledge, but they still make us think about things in new ways.

1. **A good title for this story would be:**
   a. The Answer
   b. Riddles are Not Funny
   c. Riddles
2. **How did people answer some questions years ago?**_____

   _____

3. **What is a word that means "smart"?**
   a. wise
   b. riddle
   c. answer
4. **What did people think was valuable?**_____

   _____

5. **How do riddles help people?**_____

   _____

   _____

6. **What is your favorite riddle? Why?**_____

   _____

   _____

Rule
Comprehension questions test your ability to understand what you have read.
When you understand a sentence or story, you **comprehend** it.

Read the story, then answer the questions about it.

In early times, China was divided into several states. The rulers of some states built walls around their land for protection. About two thousand years ago, Shi Huangdi became the first emperor to bring all the Chinese states together. He decided to join the walls of the old states across the northern edge of China. Shi Huangdi's wall was 6 to 15 m (20 to 50 ft) tall and 4 to 12 m (13 to 40 ft) wide. Over the next 800 years, the wall was extended and used by other emperors. After that, it was pulled apart in many places and the stones were used to build homes. From 1368 to 1644, the wall was repaired and still stands in China today. The Great Wall of China is nearly 2,400 km (1,500 mi) long and can be seen from the moon!

1. **A good title for this story would be:**
   a. The Great Wall of China
   b. Emperor Shi Huangdi
   c. Walls

2. **What did the early Chinese people build to protect their states?**

   _____

3. **What is a word that means "to make longer"?**
   a. repair
   b. extend
   c. emperor

4. **How tall is the Great Wall of China?**

   _____

5. **When the wall was torn down in places, how were the stones used?**

   _____

   _____

6. **Do you think the Great Wall still protects China? Explain.**

   _____

   _____

Rule

Comprehension questions test your ability to understand what you have read. When you understand a sentence or story, you **comprehend** it.

Read the story, then answer the questions about it.

The pitch of a sound is how high or low the sound is. Birds generally make high-pitched sounds. The bang of a drum and a man's deep voice are low-pitched sounds. What makes these sounds different? Sound is made from vibrations, or back-and-forth movements. Vibrations travel outward in waves, like ripples on water. These waves carry the vibrations through the air to our ears. The faster something vibrates, the higher the pitch. The slower it vibrates, the lower the pitch. For example, stretch a rubber band between your fingers and then pluck it. The more it is stretched the faster the vibrations and the higher the pitch it makes. The looser it becomes, the slower the vibrations and the lower the pitch.

1. **A good title for this story would be:**
   a. What is Pitch?
   b. Playing the Rubber Band
   c. Vibrations Make Noise

2. **What two things named in the story have a low pitch?** _____

   _____

3. **What is a word that means "back-and-forth movement"?**
   a. pitch
   b. vibration
   c. sound

4. **What gives a noise a high pitch?** _____

   _____

5. **Name three sounds not in the story that have a low pitch:** _____

   _____

   _____

6. **Do you prefer sounds with a high pitch or a low pitch? Explain.** _____

   _____

Rule
Comprehension questions test your ability to understand what you have read.
When you understand a sentence or story, you **comprehend** it.

Read the letter below, then answer the questions about it.

April 14

Dear Christina,

   I am so glad you came to visit my family for two weeks. Having you here was kind of like having a sister for a while! It was especially nice to have you here for my birthday. Thanks again for the neat game. I really like it! It was fun to go roller-skating together and I really liked having you come to school with me. Maybe I can come and visit your school this fall. My mom hasn't agreed yet, but she hasn't said "no" either. I know that you were disappointed when the pictures were not developed before you left, so I sent a copy of them to you with this letter. Do you like them? My favorite is the one where we are standing together at the skating rink. I think we look like twins, don't you? Write back soon. I miss you.

                              Your friend,
                              Marsha

1. **What is the purpose of this letter?** _____

   _____

   _____

2. **What is a word that means "to say yes"?**
   a. agree
   b. develop
   c. twins
3. **Name two things the girls did together during the visit:** _____

   _____

   _____

4. **Which picture was Marsha's favorite?**_____

   _____

   _____

5. **Who would you most like to visit? Explain why.** _____

   _____

   _____

> **Rule**
> **Comprehension** questions test your ability to understand what you have read.
> When you understand a sentence or story, you **comprehend** it.

Read the letter below, then answer the questions about it.

September 19

Dear Sir or Madam:

    I am doing a math project at school, and I need your help. I really like your candy and enjoy eating the five colors in each bag (red, green, purple, yellow, and orange). I have purchased 15 bags of candy and will keep a chart showing how many candies of each color are in each bag (this is a "frequency distribution"). I predicted that there will be more red than any other color, because I usually find a lot of them in the bags I eat. I would like to know how you choose the colors that go into each bag. Do you have a taste test to see which color people like best? Is there supposed to be the same number of each color in every bag? Thank you for any information you can send to me.

A good customer,
Kevin

1. **What is the purpose of this letter?** _____

_____

_____

2. **What is a word that means "to guess what will happen"?**
   a. chart
   b. predict
   c. information

3. **Who is doing the "frequency distribution" project and for which class?** ____

_____

_____

4. **How many candy colors are in each bag? What are they?** _____

_____

_____

5. **What other question might Kevin ask this company? Explain why.** _____

_____

_____

Rule

Comprehension questions test your ability to understand what you have read.
When you understand a sentence or story, you **comprehend** it.

Read the letter below, then answer the questions about it.

May 30

Dear Uncle Mark,

    Here I am in Ireland at last! I have been here one week and am having a great time. We landed at Shannon Airport and spent the first night in the town of Bunratty. There is a castle in that town and we went to a feast, or huge dinner, just like the kings of long ago would have given. We drank mead, a drink made from honey, and ate lots of good foods. There were no forks back in the days of kings, so we ate most of the meal with our fingers. My favorite was the leek and potato soup which we drank straight from the bowls. On the way back to our hotel we were driving down a narrow road. As we came around a corner, we had to stop because a whole herd of cattle was coming down the road straight at us! I sure wish you were here to see this. I will write more soon.

Your niece,
Grace

1. **What is the purpose of this letter?** _____
_____
_____

2. **What is a word that means "a drink made from honey"?**
   a. feast
   b. dagger
   c. mead
3. **Where is Grace?** _____
_____
_____

4. **What was unusual about the ride back to the hotel?** _____
_____
_____

5. **Which foreign country would you like to visit? Why?** _____
_____
_____

Rule

A **common noun** is a word that names any person, place, or thing.
A **proper noun** names a specific person, place, or thing.

Common noun – girl

Proper noun – Susan

Underline all the nouns in each sentence. Identify the nouns as either common or proper by writing **C** under the common nouns and **P** under the proper nouns.

1. Thomas Alva Edison was a great inventor.

2. We stayed in a lodge in Minnesota.

3. The books are on the shelves.

4. We saw that advertisement on television.

5. The bride walked down the aisle of the church.

6. The soldier fired the cannon at the fort.

7. The narrator, Mr. Oakley, told the story.

8. The teacher handed out a packet of papers.

9. My brother gets into a lot of mischief.

10. Was the moth eating holes in your jacket?

11. The pilot said we are going to land in Atlanta, Georgia soon.

12. Mr. Burn's dog, Rusty, won a ribbon at the Middleville Dog Show!

Rule

A **common noun** is a word that names any person, place, or thing.
A **proper noun** names a specific person, place, or thing.

Common noun – girl

Proper noun – Susan

Underline all the nouns in each sentence. Identify the nouns as either common or proper by writing **C** under the common nouns and **P** under the proper nouns.

1. The tourist took a lot of pictures in New York.

2. The explorers lit the torch as they entered the cave.

3. The solution to the puzzle was hard!

4. The operator dialed the number for my friend in Oregon.

5. It took a lot of lumber to build the house.

6. The Tate Gallery was filled with art.

7. We had a bowl of cereal for breakfast.

8. Jose is my classmate in school.

9. The ostrich is a very large bird!

10. The hunter set a snare for the rabbit.

11. Orion is a constellation in the night sky.

12. Mr. Roberts drives our bus.

Rule

A **common noun** is a word that names any person, place, or thing.
A **proper noun** names a specific person, place, or thing.

Common noun – girl
Proper noun – Susan

Underline all the nouns in each sentence. Identify the nouns as either common or proper by writing **C** under the common nouns and **P** under the proper nouns.

1. The scent of roses drifted in through the open window.

2. Our neighbor, Mr. Marsh, wore a robe over his pajamas.

3. We picked delicious fruit at Blake's Orchard.

4. Jude caught all those fish in that lagoon.

5. Ms. Greene, an architect, drew plans for the new house.

6. The farmer plowed the cornfield today.

7. Turn off the faucet after washing your hands.

8. Maria has a tiny row of freckles across her cheeks.

9. Every day I rise at daybreak.

10. I have tickets to see the Miami Dolphins' last game of the year.

11. The children enjoy swimming in Deidra's pool.

12. I saw a flock of geese flying south for the winter.

Rule
A **common noun** is a word that names any person, place, or thing. A **proper noun** names a specific person, place, or thing. <div align="center">Common noun – girl Proper noun – Susan</div>

Underline all the nouns in each sentence. Identify the nouns as either common or proper by writing **C** under the common nouns and **P** under the proper nouns.

1. Brian poured his coffee into the mug.

2. The slope was very steep!

3. Denise sat on the terrace and enjoyed the sun.

4. In Alaska, we heard wolves howling at the moon.

5. The nurse put on her uniform for work.

6. A small sparrow flew from the nest.

7. Mr. Parmenter, the librarian, put the books back on the shelves.

8. His nephew, Jake, is ten years old.

9. The sun burned brightly on the horizon.

10. I saw my image in the mirror.

11. The taxi took us across town to Bradford Avenue.

12. Mrs. Pickford moved from Chicago to Dallas.

Name _____

Rule
A **pronoun** is a word that takes the place of a noun.
I, me, you, we, they, and *it* are pronouns.

Complete each sentence by choosing the correct pronoun and writing it in the blank

1. _____ went to the dance last night.
         I   **Me**

2. _____ have dirty shoes.
       You   **It**

3. _____ won the championship.
       They   **Me**

4. Brian and Sue played together. _____ had fun.
                                     They   **We**

5. Susan opened the door and then _____ looked out.
                                       she   **he**

6. Wednesday was no fun because _____ rained all day.
                                     they   **it**

7. Mrs. Plum would like _____ to sit down now.
                            you   **he**

8. Kaye's class put on a play for _____ .
                            us   **I**

9. Roses are my favorite flower because _____ smell nice.
                                     they   **he**

10. Janice and I are eating. _____ will be finished soon.
                       We   **Us**

Rule
A **pronoun** is a word that takes the place of a noun.
I, me, you, we, they, and *it* are pronouns.

Complete each sentence by choosing the correct pronoun and writing it in the blank.

1. _____ are in the pool.
   They   **I**

2. _____ owns that old grey car.
      He   **Me**

3. _____ is a very nice girl.
         He   **She**

4. _____ must take this test myself.
      I   **We**

5. The book fell to the floor. _____ made a loud noise.
                     It   **He**

6. Jane said that _____ forgot her jacket.
                  she   **we**

7. Do _____ think it is a good picture?
         you   **she**

8. My parents are home. _____ couldn't come tonight.
               They   **He**

9. Ken and I are playing ball. _____ throw hard!
                  We   **They**

10. _____ is my best friend.
         She   **You**

Name _____

> **Rule**
> A **pronoun** is a word that takes the place of a noun.
> *I, me, you, we, they,* and *it* are pronouns.

Complete each sentence by choosing the correct pronoun and writing it in the blank.

1. Will you join _____ for lunch?
   you   **me**

2. _____ am going to school now.
   I   **He**

3. John stays late at work. _____mops the floors.
   He   **I**

4. Jody's family went to Texas. _____ are on vacation.
   They   **Us**

5. Ned said _____ likes to play chess.
   you   **he**

6. Please pass the butter to _____ .
   I   **me**

7. That newspaper was edited by _____ .
   us   **we**

8. Emily wrote a poem. _____ is about trees.
   It   **He**

9. The water in the teakettle boiled. _____ was hot!
   You   **It**

10. John gave his jacket to Ellen. _____ was a gentleman!
    She   **He**

Name _____

Rule

A **pronoun** is a word that takes the place of a noun.

I, me, you, we, they, and *it* are pronouns.

Complete each sentence by choosing the correct pronoun and writing it in the blank.

1. _____ will be getting the mail soon.

                Me   **They**

2. _____ can't be late for school.

           I   **It**

3. Wayne and Ursula are laughing because _____ are happy.

                      they   **us**

4. _____ can't decide where to have dinner.

          Us   **We**

5. Ashley is glad that _____ finished the test.

                she   **us**

6. Benjamin walks each day, but _____ never does at night.

                he   **she**

7. The plane is circling. _____ will land soon.

                She   **It**

8. The people rode on the bus. _____ were tired.

                They   **She**

9. _____ painted that picture on the wall.

         Me   **I**

10. _____ are going to bed now.

         We   **I**

Rule

An **action verb** shows action.

Jump, think, and *sleep* are action verbs.

Underline the action verb(s) in each sentence.

1. Please adjust the television picture and change the channel.

2. Janice combines the milk and eggs before she adds the flour.

3. We saluted the flag and began the program.

4. Alyssa stood at the window and watched the rain.

5. Sally requested another seat on the plane.

6. We trampled over the carpet with muddy shoes.

7. That leaky fountain squirted water on his shirt.

8. Nancy stitched the hole in the pillow.

9. The old banana rotted in the hot sun.

10. Karen predicts that it will snow tomorrow.

11. Donald paced the floor nervously.

12. Cindy fried eggs while Tyrone toasted the bread.

13. Alice chewed the meat carefully.

14. Aunt Renee washed and waxed the floor today.

Rule

An **action verb** shows action.

Jump, think, and *sleep* are action verbs.

Underline the action verb(s) in each sentence.

1. Bob recalled seeing the zebras at the zoo.

2. Thelma directs the school play each year.

3. The secretary filed the papers in the right drawer.

4. The eagle soared over the mountains.

5. Carol hitched the horse to the wagon.

6. We endanger alligators when we hunt them.

7. Sue unclasped her purse and removed her wallet.

8. Our team defeated your team last year.

9. R.J. launched the toy rocket.

10. Did the hail damage the car during the storm?

11. The peaches ripened in the warm sunshine.

12. My pencil fell off the desk and rolled across the floor.

13. The notebook caught my sleeve and tore it.

14. I packed my suitcase and carried it to the door.

Rule

An **action verb** shows action.

Jump, think, and *sleep* are action verbs.

Underline the action verb(s) in each sentence.

1. In winter, some birds migrate to warmer places.

2. Jamie scowled when she lost the contest.

3. We proceeded with the plans for Kim's surprise party.

4. We smothered the fire before we left camp.

5. Patrick scraped his knee when he fell.

6. Our choir traveled to London and sang in Hyde Park last spring.

7. Dad located Water Street on the map.

8. Candace muttered her lines in the play, so no one heard them.

9. They plunged into the water to cool themselves.

10. The woman stood and prepared to leave the meeting.

11. Jim settled into bed and turned out the light.

12. Debbie rode her bicycle to Martha's house.

13. Steve peeled the potatoes and cooked them in the pot.

14. Jody finished her homework and then called Judy.

Rule

A **linking verb** does not show action but shows a state of being. It connects the subject of a sentence to a word(s) that describes or renames the subject. Linking verbs are usually forms of *be*, such as *am, is, are, was,* and *were.*

*The cow **was** black and white.*

---

1. Mary was happy when so many people attended her dance recital.

2. Kelsey is sorry she missed the party.

3. Mysteries are my favorite type of book!

4. Today is January third.

5. We were pleased to see our team win the game.

6. Kay was amused when Ken told jokes.

7. I am anxious to finish my homework before dinner.

8. Mr. Alton was quiet during the concert.

9. The kitten was frightened when the dog barked.

10. The two little boys were happy to find the large mud puddle.

11. Nathan and I were calm during the storm, but the others were upset.

12. My favorite color is blue.

13. We are tired and want to go to bed.

14. That present is the one I brought to the party.

Name _____

Rule

An **adjective** is a word that describes a noun or a pronoun.
Playful is an adjective that could describe the noun, *puppy*.

Complete each sentence by choosing an adjective from the word box and writing it in the blank. Use each word only once.

1. The _____ grade on the test was a "B."

2. Mother made some _____ tea for my cold.

3. The new _____ penny was shiny and bright.

4. It was funny to see a _____ man at the barbershop.

5. The _____ artist drew our portrait.

6. Grandma's _____ chair was sold for a lot of money.

7. There were _____ floats in the parade.

8. The actor gave an _____ performance!

9. Those _____ flowers are blooming in my garden.

10. The _____ traveler just wanted to go to sleep.

11. Keisha and I have _____ views on which game to play.

12. That _____ quilt kept me warm all night.

WORD BOX

weary	average	incredible	antique
copper	twenty-one	bitter	bald
skillful	opposite	comfortable	violet

Name _____ Skill: Adjectives

Complete each sentence by choosing an adjective from the word box and writing it in the blank. Use each word only once.

1. Lyle had _____ ice cream for dessert.

2. The _____ doll is my favorite.

3. We had an _____ visitor in our class today.

4. The _____ child wasn't afraid of failure.

5. Mother gave me a _____ ring for my birthday.

6. The _____ weather made it difficult to drive.

7. Judd likes to listen to _____ music.

8. That _____ family won't talk to their neighbors.

9. The _____ fish was difficult to eat.

10. We had _____ bread with the spaghetti.

11. I like to have a _____ pillow on my bed.

12. The _____ lipstick was too shiny.

WORD BOX			
unexpected	vanilla	foggy	classical
bony	pearl	bold	unfriendly
plump	glossy	garlic	blue-eyed

Rule

An **adjective** is a word that describes a noun or a pronoun.
Playful is an adjective that could describe the noun, *puppy*.

Complete each sentence by choosing an adjective from the word box and writing it in the blank. Use each word only once.

1. The _____ man gave a lot of money to charity.

2. That _____ hat should be on a clown!

3. There were _____ colors from which to choose.

4. His _____ words hurt my feelings.

5. That _____ dog looks very hungry.

6. The _____ children wanted to go outside and play.

7. The _____ meat was not ready to be cooked.

8. Felicia is the _____ of the six children.

9. I had an _____ feeling I was being watched.

10. Buy _____ boots for climbing mountains.

11. We spent six _____ days in Hawaii.

12. That _____ apple should be thrown away.

WORD BOX

unkind	restless	sturdy	eerie
generous	numerous	ridiculous	frozen
rotten	eldest	glorious	skinny

Name _____   Skill: Adjectives

Rule
An **adjective** is a word that describes a noun or a pronoun.
Playful is an adjective that could describe the noun, *puppy*.

Complete each sentence by choosing an adjective from the word box and writing it in the blank. Use each word only once.

1. The _____ man bought a palace in France.

2. Caitlin wore a _____ fur to the party.

3. That _____ person was mean to the animals.

4. I've never seen anything like this. What an _____ painting!

5. I had a _____ headache last night.

6. The _____ cactus caught my jacket as I passed.

7. The _____ hamburger could not be eaten.

8. Those are _____ shoes for such a long walk.

9. Fred was the _____ person in line.

10. The _____ bread was too hard to eat.

11. The _____ woman made a mess in the kitchen.

12. I like _____ jelly on my toast.

WORD BOX			
cruel	tremendous	wealthy	sloppy
stale	raw	sensible	fake
raspberry	eighth	prickly	original

Rule
An **adverb** is a word that describes a verb or adjective. Adverbs answer the questions *where?, when?, how?,* or *to what extent?* Please speak *quietly* in the library. *Quietly* answers the question, "How should I speak in the library?"

Complete each sentence by choosing an adverb from the word box and writing it in the blank. Use each word only once.

1. The ship signaled _____ for help.

2. We walked _____ across the busy street.

3. Jessie will run _____ and warn the others.

4. Brad _____ hid the map in the bottom of a box.

5. The girl spoke _____ to her father.

6. I am glad that you are feeling _____.

7. How many pencils do I have _____ ?

8. Jacob dived _____ into the water.

9. They celebrated _____ when they won!

10. The watch was _____ expensive.

11. Mother promised that we will be leaving _____ .

12. We worked _____ all afternoon.

WORD BOX			
altogether	secretly	ahead	hard
soon	hurriedly	fearlessly	joyously
frantically	better	sweetly	very

> **Rule**
> An **adverb** is a word that describes a verb or adjective.
> Adverbs answer the questions *where?, when?, how?,* or *to what extent?*
> Please speak *quietly* in the library. *Quietly* answers the question,
> "How should I speak in the library?"

Complete each sentence by choosing an adverb from the word box and writing it in the blank. Use each word only once.

1. Howard walked _____ into the dark room.

2. We talked _____ about our plans for the party.

3. Maggie _____ patted the hurt dog.

4. I will go to the zoo _____ . I don't want to go today.

5. May we go to the movies _____ ?

6. The runners raced_____ around the track.

7. The thunder seemed to go on booming _____ .

8. T. J. threw the darts _____ at the board.

9. Please put the smelly trash can _____ .

10. I know I left that book _____ .

11. Salvator danced _____ around the room.

12. The mountain climbers are coming _____ .

WORD BOX			
bravely	gently	gracefully	wildly
somewhere	endlessly	swiftly	tomorrow
now	excitedly	down	outside

<table>
<tr><td>

Rule

An **adverb** is a word that describes a verb or adjective.
Adverbs answer the questions *where?, when?, how?,* or *to what extent?*
Please speak *quietly* in the library. *Quietly* answers the question,
"How should I speak in the library?"

</td></tr>
</table>

Complete each sentence by choosing an adverb from the word box and writing it in the blank. Use each word only once.

1. Please put all your books _____ .

2. Bob wandered _____ through the woods.

3. Hillary _____ traced the drawing.

4. Halley looked _____ at her brother.

5. Tara tiptoed _____ across the floor.

6. We should meet right _____ after lunch.

7. I got an "A" on my test _____ !

8. I have _____ wished for a million dollars.

9. We could _____ hear the train coming our way.

10. Norman _____ read the book.

11. Jason is _____ finished with dinner.

12. I need to feed all my pets _____

WORD BOX			
here	**away**	**daily**	**faintly**
carefully	**softly**	**aimlessly**	**lovingly**
often	**silently**	**yesterday**	**almost**

Name _____ Skill: Adverbs

Complete each sentence by choosing an adverb from the word box and writing it in the blank. Use each word only once.

1. We sat _____ in the sun and snoozed.

2. Corey threw the ball _____ into the air.

3. The children clattered _____ down the stairs.

4. I could _____ eat all that food!

5. Ginger always speaks _____ to her friends.

6. Everyone looked _____ as the eagle flew over.

7. The day dragged on _____ .

8. Sleepy Sandra looked _____ at her bed.

9. Carla shook her fist _____ .

10. I must get to bed early _____ !

11. Janice and Philip put the model train _____ .

12. The twins _____ waited for the plane to land.

WORD BOX			
longingly	noisily	tonight	never
anxiously	lazily	upward	together
high	endlessly	angrily	nicely

Rule

The **simple subject** is a noun or pronoun that tells whom or what the sentence is about.
The **complete subject** includes the simple subject and all the words that tell more about it.
The white cat slept on the pillow.
The simple subject is *cat* and the complete subject is *The white cat.*

Underline the complete subject of each sentence. Circle the simple subject.

1. My green and yellow ball bounced across the lawn.

2. The girl with blue ribbons in her hair is my sister.

3. The large lion roared at the tiny mouse.

4. We ate at that restaurant last week.

5. The man with the hat is my father.

6. His older sister went to Mexico.

7. The puppy with the red collar is running toward the lake.

8. The little green lizard jumped from leaf to leaf.

9. School starts next week!

10. Mr. Martinez is a great coach.

11. A salesman knocked on the front door.

12. That haircut looks very nice on you.

Write your own subject for each sentence.

1. _____ swam all day.

2. _____ drank iced tea.

3. _____ said she was tired.

4. _____ looked over her shoulder.

Rule
The **simple subject** is a noun or pronoun that tells whom or what the sentence is about. The **complete subject** includes the simple subject and all the words that tell more about it. *The white cat slept on the pillow.* The simple subject is *cat* and the complete subject is *The white cat.*

Underline the complete subject of each sentence. Circle the simple subject.

1. Uncle Brian is mailing the book to me.

2. Our class will read six books this year.

3. Turkey with stuffing is my favorite meal.

4. Harmon has to take medicine for his cold.

5. The telephone was ringing.

6. Marissa left a message on the answering machine.

7. The three-year-old child was hiding under the table.

8. Chrissy's dress with the yellow flowers was torn on the chair.

9. That brown clock is ticking too loudly!

10. The red and orange sunset was lovely.

11. Those two babies are twins.

12. The Grand Canyon is beautiful.

Write your own subject for each sentence.

1. _____ ran along the beach.

2. _____ ate too much.

3. _____ will take a nap.

4. _____ watched television.

Name _____   Skill: Subject

Rule

The **simple subject** is a noun or pronoun that tells whom or what the sentence is about.
The **complete subject** includes the simple subject and all the words that tell more about it.
The white cat slept on the pillow.
The simple subject is *cat* and the complete subject is *The white cat*.

Underline the complete subject of each sentence. Circle the simple subject.

1. The window in the hallway cracked during the storm.

2. Jason hid under his bed.

3. The hat with the red feather looks nice on you.

4. The fuzzy kittens were sitting on the couch.

5. My fingernails are getting long!

6. The newspaper was delivered early this morning.

7. The Spanish Club is taking a trip to Mexico City.

8. Marsha's hand is not as big as mine.

9. The elegant hotel had brass lamps in the lobby.

10. I would like to go now.

11. My neighbor, Mr. Green, took his son to a ball game.

12. The screaming fans enjoyed the game.

Write your own subject for each sentence.

1. _____ wrote a book.

2. _____ mowed the lawn.

3. _____ has seven pets.

4. _____ turned on the light.

Rule

The **simple subject** is a noun or pronoun that tells whom or what the sentence is about.
The **complete subject** includes the simple subject and all the words that tell more about it.
The white cat slept on the pillow.
The simple subject is *cat* and the complete subject is *The white cat.*

Underline the complete subject of each sentence. Circle the simple subject.

1. The oldest person in the room was ninety-four.

2. That old letter was written over one hundred years ago!

3. Pamela took her mother shopping.

4. The prince's horse reared and kicked its feet.

5. The post office is closed on Sunday.

6. My hungry brother ate half my ice cream.

7. The green flag belongs to my team.

8. Alphonse raced around the room.

9. The huge diamond ring sparkled in the sunlight.

10. Snow-capped mountains are beautiful.

11. The sleepy boy yawned.

12. The green goggles belong to Amy.

Write your own subject for each sentence.

1. _____ sat down on the step.

2. _____ looked at the photo.

3. _____ understood.

4. _____ cried all night.

Rule

The **simple predicate** is a verb that tells what the subject did or what was done to the subject.
The **complete predicate** includes the verb and all the words that tell more about it.
The white cat slept on the pillow.
The simple predicate is *slept* and the complete predicate is *slept on the pillow.*

Underline the complete predicate of each sentence. Circle the simple predicate.

1. The adventure began early that morning.

2. Tonya and Tony rowed the boat to shore.

3. The wind blew through the trees.

4. They live in the house on the hill.

5. The horses and cattle came back to the barn at night.

6. Mr. Weiss cracks the ice for our sodas.

7. That restaurant serves lobster.

8. Donna and Fred cooked a delicious dinner.

9. The tree grew about three feet each year.

10. Roger watches television with us.

11. Michael plays baseball with that team.

Write your own predicate for each sentence.

1. Patsy and Tom _____ .

2. The brown book _____ .

3. The computer near the window _____ .

4. Paula _____ .

Name _____

Skill: Predicate

Rule

The **simple predicate** is a verb that tells what the subject did or what was done to the subject.
The **complete predicate** includes the verb and all the words that tell more about it.

The white cat slept on the pillow.

The simple predicate is *slept* and the complete predicate is *slept on the pillow.*

Underline the complete predicate of each sentence. Circle the simple predicate.

1. Bess danced in the school play.

2. We went to the mall after the library.

3. California is a state on the west coast.

4. The weather began to turn cool.

5. It rained for hours yesterday!

6. Opal made a painting for her mom.

7. Snow fell for six hours.

8. Seven students were in the spelling bee.

9. The tractor made a loud noise.

10. We served ice cream and cake at the party.

11. The children raced to the end of the block.

Write your own predicate for each sentence.

1. The big shoes _____ .

2. My pet _____ .

3. That field _____ .

4. The largest building _____ .

> **Rule**
> The **simple predicate** is a verb that tells what the subject did or what was done to the subject.
> The **complete predicate** includes the verb and all the words that tell more about it.
> *The white cat slept on the pillow.*
> The simple predicate is *slept* and the complete predicate is *slept on the pillow.*

Underline the complete predicate of each sentence. Circle the simple predicate.

1. Aunt Tina sent a beautiful card for my birthday.

2. My dad likes to read books about history.

3. Dorothy drives a red truck.

4. Those men cut down the tall pine tree.

5. We ate popcorn during the movie.

6. The lemonade tasted sweet.

7. Judy saw exactly what happened.

8. Penny rode the black horse.

9. An old car rattled down the street.

10. Our team won the trophy!

11. The squirrel hid the acorn under the tree.

Write your own predicate for each sentence.

1. This crayon _____ .

2. I _____ .

3. The red sweater _____ .

4. Hot sand _____ .

Rule

The **simple predicate** is a verb that tells what the subject did or what was done to the subject.
The **complete predicate** includes the verb and all the words that tell more about it.
The white cat slept on the pillow.
The simple predicate is *slept* and the complete predicate is *slept on the pillow.*

Underline the complete predicate of each sentence. Circle the simple predicate.

1. Red and blue fireworks burst in the night sky.

2. The lamp fell off the table.

3. Many leaves on the trees turned red this week.

4. The brisk fall days felt chilly.

5. Jerry and Vernon went home.

6. We changed the channel at nine o'clock.

7. Alex wants another cookie.

8. The mosquito bit me on the nose.

9. Abigail and her sister told that story to the children.

10. Mike put the onions in the soup.

11. Joey and David went fishing.

Write your own predicate for each sentence.

1. The telephone _____ .

2. Your jacket _____ .

3. Fran's grandmother _____ .

4. The baby in the stroller _____ .

Name _____   Skill: Fragments

Rule

A **sentence** is a group of words that expresses a complete thought.
A **fragment** is an incomplete sentence because it does not express a complete thought.
    Fragments: *Anna and Beth.* (missing a predicate that tells what happened)
                      Went swimming. (missing a subject that tells who)
    Sentence: *Anna and Beth went swimming.*

Write **S** if the words below form a sentence and **F** if they are a fragment.

_____ 1. Into the tall grass.

_____ 2. Janice ate the cake.

_____ 3. The boy in the dark blue suit.

_____ 4. After we eat.

_____ 5. The elephants blew water out of their trunks!

_____ 6. Never went there again.

_____ 7. The beautiful lake at the bottom of the mountain.

_____ 8. Candace ate corn.

_____ 9. The small bug crawled into the crack.

_____ 10. Under the leaves we raked yesterday.

_____ 11. Donald swam all day.

_____ 12. Carol is calling us.

Add words to make each phrase a sentence.

1. Frances gathered _____ .

2. _____ clothes on the line.

3. A low rumble _____ .

4. _____ disappeared!

Rule

A **sentence** is a group of words that expresses a complete thought.
A **fragment** is an incomplete sentence because it does not express a complete thought.
  Fragments: *Anna and Beth.* (missing a predicate that tells what happened)
                Went swimming. (missing a subject that tells who)
  Sentence: *Anna and Beth went swimming.*

Write **S** if the words below form a sentence and **F** if they are a fragment.

_____ 1. Rang loudly and woke all of us!

_____ 2. Down the dark tunnel and into a large cave.

_____ 3. Pete and his cousin, Elmo.

_____ 4. We will play a game after dinner.

_____ 5. You may come along with us.

_____ 6. The darts hit the board.

_____ 7. Around the corner and over the bridge.

_____ 8. That is my house.

_____ 9. Frank ate the beans.

_____ 10. A hot dog and some potato chips.

_____ 11. She is a shy girl.

_____ 12. The states of Texas, Michigan, and New York.

Add words to make each phrase a sentence.

1. After the rainstorm we _____ .

2. _____ munching on apples.

3. Kelly _____ .

4. _____ over our heads.

Skill: Capitalization

Rule

Remember to use **capital letters** for:
- the first word in a sentence
- the pronoun "I"
- proper nouns
- important words in book and movie titles

Each sentence has one or more capitalization mistakes. Write each sentence correctly on the line below it.

1. jeff plays the piano every thursday afternoon._____

_____

2. this october, we will take a trip to williamsburg, virginia._____

_____

3. i told mrs. potter that her cat, fluffy, was on the roof again._____

_____

4. next year, i will be in the fifth grade at carver elementary school._____

_____

5. buffalo once lived in many parts of north america._____

_____

6. my aunt linda visited friends in france and italy._____

_____

7. who is pulling on my shirt?_____

_____

8. the rocky mountains are very tall and beautiful._____

_____

9. jeremy and i play clarinet in the band._____

_____

10. i would like to have a thick steak for dinner on my birthday._____

_____

11. isobel drank tea in london, england._____

_____

12. last tuesday, john broke his leg._____

_____

Rule

Remember to use **capital letters** for:
- the first word in a sentence   • the pronoun "I"
- proper nouns   • important words in book and movie titles

Each sentence has one or more capitalization mistakes. Write each sentence correctly on the line below it.

1. my friend tony and i like chocolate ice cream.

   _____

2. after school today, paul and mike will have a race.

   _____

3. i go to brandford elementary school.

   _____

4. how often does your mother take you to the mall?

   _____

5. mr. davis is the best teacher in our school.

   _____

6. myron's family just moved to lincoln, nebraska.

   _____

7. jessie played in a concert last april.

   _____

8. i am reading a book called the mysterious stranger.

   _____

9. amy and beth are two characters in the book little women.

   _____

10. the nile river flows through egypt.

    _____

11. that mummy looks a lot like king tut!

    _____

12. have you ever visited chicago?

    _____

Add.

1. 97 + 37	2. 83 + 58	3. 68 + 34	4. 56 + 92	5. 69 + 42	6. 27 + 58	7. 91 + 29
8. 46 + 57	9. 65 + 48	10. 51 + 79	11. 78 + 32	12. 63 + 78	13. 49 + 83	14. 74 + 78
15. 27 + 84	16. 47 + 76	17. 42 + 89	18. 63 + 51	19. 74 + 29	20. 92 + 76	21. 59 + 16
22. 25 + 57	23. 57 + 42	24. 64 + 57	25. 86 + 17	26. 35 + 28	27. 54 + 85	28. 17 + 66
29. 56 + 45	30. 79 + 24	31. 39 + 52	32. 58 + 43	33. 73 + 27	34. 93 + 45	35. 87 + 26
36. 84 + 26	37. 37 + 73	38. 46 + 49	39. 63 + 57	40. 84 + 34	41. 79 + 42	42. 52 + 57
43. 45 + 56	44. 59 + 33	45. 49 + 23	46. 26 + 68	47. 65 + 25	48. 86 + 48	49. 36 + 27

Name _____

Add.

1.
$$\begin{array}{r} 43 \\ + 59 \\ \hline \end{array}$$

2.
$$\begin{array}{r} 27 \\ + 55 \\ \hline \end{array}$$

3.
$$\begin{array}{r} 86 \\ + 27 \\ \hline \end{array}$$

4.
$$\begin{array}{r} 58 \\ + 46 \\ \hline \end{array}$$

5.
$$\begin{array}{r} 25 \\ + 69 \\ \hline \end{array}$$

6.
$$\begin{array}{r} 87 \\ + 44 \\ \hline \end{array}$$

7.
$$\begin{array}{r} 87 \\ + 29 \\ \hline \end{array}$$

8.
$$\begin{array}{r} 99 \\ + 29 \\ \hline \end{array}$$

9.
$$\begin{array}{r} 53 \\ + 78 \\ \hline \end{array}$$

10.
$$\begin{array}{r} 48 \\ + 67 \\ \hline \end{array}$$

11.
$$\begin{array}{r} 75 \\ + 58 \\ \hline \end{array}$$

12.
$$\begin{array}{r} 91 \\ + 39 \\ \hline \end{array}$$

13.
$$\begin{array}{r} 33 \\ + 79 \\ \hline \end{array}$$

14.
$$\begin{array}{r} 84 \\ + 87 \\ \hline \end{array}$$

15.
$$\begin{array}{r} 69 \\ + 84 \\ \hline \end{array}$$

16.
$$\begin{array}{r} 93 \\ + 88 \\ \hline \end{array}$$

17.
$$\begin{array}{r} 72 \\ + 89 \\ \hline \end{array}$$

18.
$$\begin{array}{r} 45 \\ + 78 \\ \hline \end{array}$$

19.
$$\begin{array}{r} 64 \\ + 98 \\ \hline \end{array}$$

20.
$$\begin{array}{r} 86 \\ + 36 \\ \hline \end{array}$$

21.
$$\begin{array}{r} 26 \\ + 97 \\ \hline \end{array}$$

22.
$$\begin{array}{r} 96 \\ + 58 \\ \hline \end{array}$$

23.
$$\begin{array}{r} 56 \\ + 86 \\ \hline \end{array}$$

24.
$$\begin{array}{r} 79 \\ + 38 \\ \hline \end{array}$$

25.
$$\begin{array}{r} 86 \\ + 27 \\ \hline \end{array}$$

26.
$$\begin{array}{r} 94 \\ + 47 \\ \hline \end{array}$$

27.
$$\begin{array}{r} 36 \\ + 78 \\ \hline \end{array}$$

28.
$$\begin{array}{r} 76 \\ + 45 \\ \hline \end{array}$$

29.
$$\begin{array}{r} 89 \\ + 47 \\ \hline \end{array}$$

30.
$$\begin{array}{r} 58 \\ + 62 \\ \hline \end{array}$$

31.
$$\begin{array}{r} 73 \\ + 49 \\ \hline \end{array}$$

32.
$$\begin{array}{r} 86 \\ + 76 \\ \hline \end{array}$$

33.
$$\begin{array}{r} 78 \\ + 25 \\ \hline \end{array}$$

34.
$$\begin{array}{r} 95 \\ + 61 \\ \hline \end{array}$$

35.
$$\begin{array}{r} 57 \\ + 58 \\ \hline \end{array}$$

36.
$$\begin{array}{r} 38 \\ + 87 \\ \hline \end{array}$$

37.
$$\begin{array}{r} 64 \\ + 83 \\ \hline \end{array}$$

38.
$$\begin{array}{r} 69 \\ + 52 \\ \hline \end{array}$$

39.
$$\begin{array}{r} 77 \\ + 54 \\ \hline \end{array}$$

40.
$$\begin{array}{r} 93 \\ + 58 \\ \hline \end{array}$$

41.
$$\begin{array}{r} 65 \\ + 43 \\ \hline \end{array}$$

42.
$$\begin{array}{r} 79 \\ + 79 \\ \hline \end{array}$$

43.
$$\begin{array}{r} 56 \\ + 77 \\ \hline \end{array}$$

44.
$$\begin{array}{r} 77 \\ + 64 \\ \hline \end{array}$$

45.
$$\begin{array}{r} 85 \\ + 68 \\ \hline \end{array}$$

46.
$$\begin{array}{r} 27 \\ + 87 \\ \hline \end{array}$$

47.
$$\begin{array}{r} 89 \\ + 23 \\ \hline \end{array}$$

48.
$$\begin{array}{r} 58 \\ + 44 \\ \hline \end{array}$$

49.
$$\begin{array}{r} 93 \\ + 28 \\ \hline \end{array}$$

Add.

1.	2.	3.	4.	5.	6.	7.
358	371	408	327	417	730	344
+ 227	+ 389	+ 159	+ 196	+ 125	+ 197	+ 523

8.	9.	10.	11.	12.	13.	14.
751	400	111	250	219	382	348
+ 225	+ 127	+ 345	+ 178	+ 470	+ 160	+ 436

15.	16.	17.	18.	19.	20.	21.
709	522	398	270	520	254	331
+ 189	+ 157	+ 145	+ 134	+ 177	+ 384	+ 245

22.	23.	24.	25.	26.	27.	28.
428	197	724	181	533	451	613
+ 150	+ 402	+ 150	+ 199	+ 238	+ 315	+ 178

29.	30.	31.	32.	33.	34.	35.
357	519	834	313	558	687	901
+ 417	+ 170	+ 196	+ 488	+ 184	+ 139	+149

36.	37.	38.	39.	40.	41.	42.
410	737	426	166	404	259	272
+ 291	+288	+ 497	+ 617	+ 395	+ 450	+ 438

43.	44.	45.	46.	47.	48.	49.
106	857	849	426	572	553	295
+ 329	+341	+ 254	+ 208	+ 259	+ 347	+ 486

Name _____ Skill: Subtraction of One and Two Digits

Subtract.

1.	2.	3.	4.	5.	6.	7.
3 − 2	7 − 0	9 − 4	7 − 3	8 − 8	5 − 2	9 − 4

8.	9.	10.	11.	12.	13.	14.
4 − 2	9 − 7	10 − 4	6 − 1	9 − 8	2 − 1	8 − 3

15.	16.	17.	18.	19.	20.	21.
10 − 9	12 − 5	11 − 4	10 − 7	2 − 2	15 − 6	13 − 8

22.	23.	24.	25.	26.	27.	28.
8 − 4	7 − 2	14 − 5	11 − 9	17 − 9	5 − 3	13 − 6

29.	30.	31.	32.	33.	34.	35.
14 − 6	9 − 9	14 − 7	13 − 9	8 − 2	12 − 9	16 − 7

36.	37.	38.	39.	40.	41.	42.
10 − 2	18 − 9	12 − 5	16 − 7	14 − 5	9 − 7	17 − 8

43.	44.	45.	46.	47.	48.	49.
10 − 6	7 − 6	9 − 6	6 − 2	15 − 8	15 − 6	16 − 8

Subtract.

1.	2.	3.	4.	5.	6.	7.
30 − 10	70 − 40	90 − 40	60 − 30	80 − 80	50 − 20	90 − 10

8.	9.	10.	11.	12.	13.	14.
40 − 20	90 − 70	50 − 40	60 − 10	90 − 80	20 − 10	80 − 30

15.	16.	17.	18.	19.	20.	21.
55 − 43	72 − 50	88 − 41	33 − 22	72 − 32	75 − 64	99 − 48

22.	23.	24.	25.	26.	27.	28.
87 − 46	78 − 24	83 − 51	69 − 19	76 − 45	58 − 30	66 − 62

29.	30.	31.	32.	33.	34.	35.
72 − 61	98 − 46	33 − 12	84 − 23	88 − 72	48 − 32	76 − 51

36.	37.	38.	39.	40.	41.	42.
95 − 23	80 − 40	67 − 51	82 − 70	96 − 53	79 − 17	87 − 47

43.	44.	45.	46.	47.	48.	49.
80 − 60	70 − 60	93 − 60	57 − 23	77 − 17	84 − 62	93 − 71

Subtract.

1. 91 −56	**2.** 52 −49	**3.** 43 −38	**4.** 71 −34	**5.** 75 −46	**6.** 84 −47	**7.** 61 −12
8. 86 −58	**9.** 90 −29	**10.** 42 −28	**11.** 94 −66	**12.** 62 −49	**13.** 55 −17	**14.** 41 −25
15. 86 −39	**16.** 34 −18	**17.** 73 −38	**18.** 44 −15	**19.** 73 −25	**20.** 58 −39	**21.** 52 −24
22. 38 −19	**23.** 46 −28	**24.** 53 −28	**25.** 95 −48	**26.** 84 −27	**27.** 64 −39	**28.** 92 −59
29. 87 −38	**30.** 74 −25	**31.** 67 −38	**32.** 71 −64	**33.** 83 −28	**34.** 41 −34	**35.** 71 −42
36. 93 −75	**37.** 84 −19	**38.** 82 −73	**39.** 84 −37	**40.** 66 −48	**41.** 75 −27	**42.** 54 −39
43. 75 −17	**44.** 47 −18	**45.** 40 −29	**46.** 61 −23	**47.** 54 −38	**48.** 81 −27	**49.** 67 −38

Name _____   Skill: Subtraction of Three Digits

Subtract.

1.	2.	3.	4.	5.	6.	7.
326 − 285	972 − 609	685 − 246	518 − 329	741 − 362	438 − 258	371 − 283

8.	9.	10.	11.	12.	13.	14.
529 − 482	625 − 407	514 − 126	664 − 278	742 − 467	200 − 158	634 − 277

15.	16.	17.	18.	19.	20.	21.
423 − 285	222 − 153	435 − 166	628 − 499	757 − 178	637 − 388	423 − 285

22.	23.	24.	25.	26.	27.	28.
533 − 240	415 − 196	382 − 175	632 − 377	585 − 423	778 − 439	130 − 115

29.	30.	31.	32.	33.	34.	35.
623 − 194	900 − 309	722 − 317	377 − 186	871 − 384	628 − 300	454 − 279

36.	37.	38.	39.	40.	41.	42.
990 − 731	818 − 693	572 − 335	951 − 357	825 − 469	771 − 217	943 − 761

43.	44.	45.	46.	47.	48.	49.
407 − 328	431 − 298	906 − 682	486 − 297	615 − 288	883 − 227	631 − 156

Multiply.

1.	2.	3.	4.	5.	6.	7.
3 $\times 2$	7 $\times 0$	9 $\times 3$	3 $\times 1$	8 $\times 2$	5 $\times 2$	3 $\times 7$

8.	9.	10.	11.	12.	13.	14.
1 $\times 2$	0 $\times 8$	3 $\times 4$	2 $\times 9$	9 $\times 0$	2 $\times 1$	8 $\times 3$

15.	16.	17.	18.	19.	20.	21.
9 $\times 1$	6 $\times 3$	0 $\times 4$	5 $\times 1$	2 $\times 2$	5 $\times 3$	3 $\times 2$

22.	23.	24.	25.	26.	27.	28.
8 $\times 0$	8 $\times 3$	1 $\times 5$	3 $\times 9$	9 $\times 2$	5 $\times 0$	3 $\times 6$

29.	30.	31.	32.	33.	34.	35.
6 $\times 0$	9 $\times 3$	1 $\times 7$	3 $\times 3$	8 $\times 2$	2 $\times 1$	7 $\times 2$

36.	37.	38.	39.	40.	41.	42.
10 $\times 2$	0 $\times 9$	2 $\times 0$	3 $\times 5$	0 $\times 1$	3 $\times 9$	8 $\times 2$

43.	44.	45.	46.	47.	48.	49.
6 $\times 3$	7 $\times 1$	2 $\times 6$	4 $\times 2$	5 $\times 0$	1 $\times 4$	10 $\times 6$

Multiply.

1. 10   2.   7   3.   6   4.   3   5.   8   6. 11   7.   3
   x 4   x 5   x 3   x 7   x 5   x 2   x 6

8.   1   9.   0   10. 6   11. 10   12. 9   13. 5   14. 8
   x 4   x 5   x 4   x 9   x 4   x 1   x 6

15. 9   16. 11   17. 0   18. 5   19. 4   20. 5   21. 3
   x 4   x 5   x 6   x 7   x 2   x 5   x 6

22. 11   23. 8   24. 1   25. 6   26. 9   27. 5   28. 6
   x 7   x 4   x 5   x 9   x 7   x 4   x 6

29. 6   30. 9   31. 4   32. 3   33. 10   34. 2   35. 7
   x 6   x 5   x 7   x 7   x 5   x 4   x 7

36. 10   37. 4   38. 5   39. 8   40. 6   41. 11   42. 7
   x 4   x 1   x 0   x 5   x 1   x 6   x 9

43. 6   44. 7   45. 7   46. 10   47. 5   48. 7   49. 11
   x 7   x 7   x 6   x 2   x 6   x 4   x 3

Name _____ Skill: Multiplication Facts through Twelve

Multiply.

1.	2.	3.	4.	5.	6.	7.
8 x 3	7 x 9	10 x 3	11 x 3	8 x 8	9 x 2	10 x 7

8.	9.	10.	11.	12.	13.	14.
12 x 2	10 x 8	9 x 4	8 x 9	10 x 9	12 x 1	8 x 3

15.	16.	17.	18.	19.	20.	21.
12 x 9	6 x 9	10 x 4	12 x 5	10 x 2	8 x 3	9 x 8

22.	23.	24.	25.	26.	27.	28.
11 x 0	8 x 3	12 x 5	7 x 8	9 x 9	10 x 3	11 x 6

29.	30.	31.	32.	33.	34.	35.
10 x 6	9 x 3	11 x 7	3 x 8	8 x 8	10 x 2	7 x 9

36.	37.	38.	39.	40.	41.	42.
11 x 2	10 x 9	2 x 9	8 x 5	10 x 1	11 x 9	10 x 7

43.	44.	45.	46.	47.	48.	49.
11 x 6	7 x 8	10 x 6	12 x 6	5 x 9	9 x 4	12 x 6

Divide.

1.
$2\overline{)18}$

2.
$3\overline{)9}$

3.
$3\overline{)24}$

4.
$1\overline{)4}$

5.
$2\overline{)8}$

6.
$3\overline{)15}$

7.
$4\overline{)32}$

8.
$1\overline{)12}$

9.
$3\overline{)3}$

10.
$2\overline{)20}$

11.
$4\overline{)16}$

12.
$3\overline{)36}$

13.
$1\overline{)2}$

14.
$4\overline{)44}$

15.
$2\overline{)2}$

16.
$1\overline{)8}$

17.
$2\overline{)6}$

18.
$3\overline{)21}$

19.
$4\overline{)12}$

20.
$3\overline{)27}$

21.
$4\overline{)8}$

22.
$1\overline{)10}$

23.
$2\overline{)24}$

24.
$2\overline{)4}$

25.
$3\overline{)30}$

26.
$4\overline{)48}$

27.
$3\overline{)33}$

28.
$4\overline{)24}$

29.
$2\overline{)14}$

30.
$4\overline{)20}$

Divide.

1.
$5\overline{)15}$

2.
$6\overline{)42}$

3.
$7\overline{)7}$

4.
$6\overline{)12}$

5.
$8\overline{)96}$

6.
$5\overline{)30}$

7.
$7\overline{)35}$

8.
$5\overline{)40}$

9.
$8\overline{)24}$

10.
$6\overline{)60}$

11.
$6\overline{)18}$

12.
$7\overline{)63}$

13.
$5\overline{)5}$

14.
$8\overline{)72}$

15.
$6\overline{)36}$

16.
$8\overline{)80}$

17.
$5\overline{)60}$

18.
$7\overline{)28}$

19.
$6\overline{)66}$

20.
$7\overline{)14}$

21.
$5\overline{)35}$

22.
$6\overline{)6}$

23.
$8\overline{)48}$

24.
$5\overline{)50}$

25.
$8\overline{)88}$

26.
$8\overline{)32}$

27.
$5\overline{)45}$

28.
$7\overline{)77}$

29.
$8\overline{)64}$

30.
$6\overline{)48}$

Divide.

1.

$9\overline{)90}$

2.

$10\overline{)20}$

3.

$11\overline{)99}$

4.

$12\overline{)108}$

5.

$11\overline{)77}$

6.

$12\overline{)24}$

7.

$10\overline{)60}$

8.

$12\overline{)60}$

9.

$11\overline{)110}$

10.

$10\overline{)100}$

11.

$9\overline{)27}$

12.

$9\overline{)9}$

13.

$10\overline{)120}$

14.

$11\overline{)121}$

15.

$9\overline{)108}$

16.

$1\overline{)8}$

17.

$2\overline{)6}$

18.

$3\overline{)21}$

19.

$4\overline{)12}$

20.

$3\overline{)27}$

21.

$9\overline{)36}$

22.

$10\overline{)40}$

23.

$12\overline{)36}$

24.

$11\overline{)132}$

25.

$9\overline{)36}$

26.

$9\overline{)45}$

27.

$11\overline{)44}$

28.

$12\overline{)144}$

29.

$10\overline{)110}$

30.

$11\overline{)121}$

Name _____

Use the given number to find the place values. The first one has been done for you.

1. The number is:

7,320,194.685

    a. Name the digit in the tens place. _____ **9** _____
    b. Name the digit in the tenths place. _____
    c. Name the digit in the millions place. _____
    d. Name the digit in the ones place. _____
    e. In what place value is the digit "0"? _____
    f. In what place value is the digit "4"? _____
    g. In what place value is the digit "3"? _____
    h. In what place value is the digit "5"? _____

2. The number is:

8,635.147

    a. Name the digit in the hundreds place. _____
    b. Name the digit in the hundredths place. _____
    c. Name the digit in the thousands place. _____
    d. Name the digit in the tenths place. _____
    e. Name the number that is one hundred more. _____
    f. Name the number that is one thousand less. _____
    g. Name the number that is one-hundredth less. _____
    h. Name the number that is one more. _____

3. The number is:

1,320,796.485

    a. Name the digit in the millions place. _____
    b. Name the digit in the ones place. _____
    c. Name the digit in the thousandths place. _____
    d. Name the digit in the ten thousands place. _____
    e. Name the number that is ten thousand less. _____
    f. Name the number that is one-thousandth more. _____
    g. Name the number that is one less. _____
    h. Name the number that is one million more. _____

Name _____   Skill: Place Value

Use the given number to find the place values. The first one has been done for you.

1. The number is:

    | **453,621.908** |

    a. Name the digit in the thousands place. _____**3**_____
    b. Name the digit in the hundredths place. _____
    c. Name the digit in the ten thousands place. _____
    d. Name the digit in the ones place. _____
    e. In what place value is the digit "8"? _____
    f. In what place value is the digit "4"? _____
    g. In what place value is the digit "9"? _____
    h. In what place value is the digit "5"? _____

2. The number is:

    | **45,923.0168** |

    a. Name the digit in the hundreds place. _____
    b. Name the digit in the hundredths place. _____
    c. Name the digit in the thousands place. _____
    d. Name the digit in the thousandths place. _____
    e. Name the number that is ten more. _____
    f. Name the number that is one thousand less. _____
    g. Name the number that is one-hundredth less. _____
    h. Name the number that is one more. _____

3. The number is:

    | **5,023,178.496** |

    a. Name the digit in the millions place. _____
    b. Name the digit in the ones place. _____
    c. Name the digit in the hundredths place. _____
    d. Name the digit in the hundred thousands place. _____
    e. Name the number that is ten thousand less. _____
    f. Name the number that is one-thousandth more. _____
    g. Name the number that is one less. _____
    h. Name the number that is one million more. _____

1. Round these numbers to the nearest ten. The first one has been done for you.

a. 23 _____20_____   f. 48 _____

b. 59 _____   g. 96 _____

c. 237 _____   h. 151 _____

d. 468 _____   i. 375 _____

e. 783 _____   j. 994 _____

2. Round these numbers to the nearest hundred. The first one has been done for you.

a. 749 _____700_____   k. 637 _____

b. 291 _____   l. 590 _____

c. 453 _____   m. 849 _____

d. 1,658 _____   n. 5,267 _____

e. 3,409 _____   o. 3,721 _____

f. 872 _____   p. 75 _____

g. 7,433 _____   q. 382 _____

h. 6,551 _____   r. 5,098 _____

i. 3,929 _____   s. 4,629 _____

j. 8,494 _____   t. 9,712 _____

3. Round these numbers to the nearest thousand. The first one has been done for you.

a. 2,282 _____2,000_____   f. 4,503 _____

b. 5,499 _____   g. 8,457 _____

c. 7,911 _____   h. 6,386 _____

d. 17,695 _____   i. 14,623 _____

e. 20,392 _____   j. 19,821 _____

1. Round these numbers to the nearest ten. The first one has been done for you.

a. 13 _____10_____   f. 16 _____

b. 48 _____   g. 25 _____

c. 79 _____   h. 78 _____

d. 231 _____   i. 307 _____

e. 965 _____   j. 797 _____

2. Round these numbers to the nearest hundred. The first one has been done for you.

a. 71 _____100_____   k. 32 _____

b. 43 _____   l. 157 _____

c. 429 _____   m. 629 _____

d. 589 _____   n. 572 _____

e. 848 _____   o. 4,263 _____

f. 546 _____   p. 728 _____

g. 971 _____   q. 939 _____

h. 2,836 _____   r. 6,543 _____

i. 5,889 _____   s. 9,714 _____

j. 8,417 _____   t. 10,556 _____

3. Round these numbers to the nearest thousand. The first one has been done for you.

a. 374 _____0_____   f. 801 _____

b. 2,068 _____   g. 2,560 _____

c. 3,722 _____   h. 6,917 _____

d. 8,968 _____   i. 9,543 _____

e. 21,743 _____   j. 42,198 _____

Name _____   Skill: Fraction Addition

Add. Write each answer in simplest form. The first one has been done for you.

1. $\dfrac{1}{6} + \dfrac{1}{6} = \boxed{\dfrac{1}{3}}$

2. $\dfrac{3}{5} + \dfrac{1}{5} = \boxed{}$

3. $\dfrac{1}{7} + \dfrac{3}{7} = \boxed{}$

4. $\dfrac{6}{7} + \dfrac{3}{7} = \boxed{}$

5. $\dfrac{1}{8} + \dfrac{4}{8} = \boxed{}$

6. $\dfrac{2}{9} + \dfrac{5}{9} = \boxed{}$

7. $\dfrac{5}{9} + \dfrac{1}{9} = \boxed{}$

8. $\dfrac{2}{5} + \dfrac{3}{5} = \boxed{}$

9. $\dfrac{1}{7} + \dfrac{4}{7} = \boxed{}$

10. $\dfrac{2}{4} + \dfrac{1}{4} = \boxed{}$

11. $\dfrac{1}{3} + \dfrac{1}{3} = \boxed{}$

12. $\dfrac{1}{6} + \dfrac{3}{6} = \boxed{}$

13. $\dfrac{2}{5} + \dfrac{2}{5} = \boxed{}$

14. $\dfrac{5}{7} + \dfrac{1}{7} = \boxed{}$

15. $\dfrac{2}{9} + \dfrac{3}{9} = \boxed{}$

16. $\dfrac{4}{8} + \dfrac{2}{8} = \boxed{}$

Skill: Fraction Addition

Add. Write each answer in simplest form. The first one has been done for you.

1. $\frac{2}{5} + \frac{1}{5} = \boxed{\frac{3}{5}}$

2. $\frac{3}{5} + \frac{1}{5} = \boxed{}$

3. $\frac{7}{9} + \frac{1}{9} = \boxed{}$

4. $\frac{1}{5} + \frac{2}{5} = \boxed{}$

5. $\frac{3}{8} + \frac{4}{8} = \boxed{}$

6. $\frac{5}{7} + \frac{1}{7} = \boxed{}$

7. $\frac{5}{6} + \frac{2}{6} = \boxed{}$

8. $\frac{1}{9} + \frac{2}{9} = \boxed{}$

9. $\frac{1}{4} + \frac{3}{4} = \boxed{}$

10. $\frac{3}{4} + \frac{1}{4} = \boxed{}$

11. $\frac{1}{6} + \frac{5}{6} = \boxed{}$

12. $\frac{5}{6} + \frac{1}{6} = \boxed{}$

13. $\frac{1}{3} + \frac{2}{3} = \boxed{}$

14. $\frac{2}{3} + \frac{3}{3} = \boxed{}$

15. $\frac{1}{8} + \frac{1}{8} = \boxed{}$

16. $\frac{5}{8} + \frac{1}{8} = \boxed{}$

Subtract. Write each answer in simplest form. The first one has been done for you.

1. $\dfrac{2}{3} - \dfrac{1}{3} = \boxed{\dfrac{1}{3}}$

2. $\dfrac{7}{9} - \dfrac{5}{9} = \boxed{}$

3. $\dfrac{3}{7} - \dfrac{1}{7} = \boxed{}$

4. $\dfrac{3}{5} - \dfrac{1}{5} = \boxed{}$

5. $\dfrac{5}{8} - \dfrac{2}{8} = \boxed{}$

6. $\dfrac{3}{4} - \dfrac{1}{4} = \boxed{}$

7. $\dfrac{8}{9} - \dfrac{3}{9} = \boxed{}$

8. $\dfrac{4}{6} - \dfrac{2}{6} = \boxed{}$

9. $\dfrac{6}{7} - \dfrac{4}{7} = \boxed{}$

10. $\dfrac{5}{7} - \dfrac{1}{7} = \boxed{}$

11. $\dfrac{8}{9} - \dfrac{1}{9} = \boxed{}$

12. $\dfrac{6}{8} - \dfrac{1}{8} = \boxed{}$

13. $\dfrac{4}{5} - \dfrac{2}{5} = \boxed{}$

14. $\dfrac{2}{3} - \dfrac{2}{3} = \boxed{}$

15. $\dfrac{8}{9} - \dfrac{3}{9} = \boxed{}$

16. $\dfrac{7}{9} - \dfrac{1}{9} = \boxed{}$

Name _____   Skill: Fraction Subtraction

Subtract. Write each answer in simplest form. The first one has been done for you.

1. $\dfrac{12}{13} - \dfrac{11}{13} = \boxed{\dfrac{1}{13}}$

2. $\dfrac{5}{5} - \dfrac{2}{5} = \boxed{}$

3. $\dfrac{7}{7} - \dfrac{4}{7} = \boxed{}$

4. $\dfrac{8}{9} - \dfrac{4}{9} = \boxed{}$

5. $\dfrac{6}{8} - \dfrac{3}{8} = \boxed{}$

6. $\dfrac{3}{4} - \dfrac{2}{4} = \boxed{}$

7. $\dfrac{8}{9} - \dfrac{1}{9} = \boxed{}$

8. $\dfrac{6}{6} - \dfrac{5}{6} = \boxed{}$

9. $\dfrac{5}{7} - \dfrac{2}{7} = \boxed{}$

10. $\dfrac{4}{7} - \dfrac{2}{7} = \boxed{}$

11. $\dfrac{8}{9} - \dfrac{7}{9} = \boxed{}$

12. $\dfrac{5}{6} - \dfrac{2}{6} = \boxed{}$

13. $\dfrac{2}{6} - \dfrac{1}{6} = \boxed{}$

14. $\dfrac{5}{7} - \dfrac{1}{7} = \boxed{}$

15. $\dfrac{3}{4} - \dfrac{1}{4} = \boxed{}$

16. $\dfrac{7}{8} - \dfrac{3}{8} = \boxed{}$

Name _____ Skill: Less than, Greater than, Equal to

Compare the fractions. Write <, >, or = in each square to make a true math statement. The first one has been done for you.

1. $\dfrac{1}{2}$ $\boxed{=}$ $\dfrac{6}{12}$

2. $\dfrac{3}{4}$ $\boxed{}$ $\dfrac{1}{4}$

3. $\dfrac{1}{4}$ $\boxed{}$ $\dfrac{5}{10}$

4. $\dfrac{1}{3}$ $\boxed{}$ $\dfrac{5}{6}$

5. $\dfrac{2}{3}$ $\boxed{}$ $\dfrac{5}{6}$

6. $\dfrac{4}{8}$ $\boxed{}$ $\dfrac{1}{3}$

7. $\dfrac{4}{5}$ $\boxed{}$ $\dfrac{7}{10}$

8. $\dfrac{4}{9}$ $\boxed{}$ $\dfrac{1}{2}$

9. $\dfrac{3}{9}$ $\boxed{}$ $\dfrac{1}{3}$

10. $\dfrac{5}{6}$ $\boxed{}$ $\dfrac{2}{3}$

11. $\dfrac{2}{8}$ $\boxed{}$ $\dfrac{2}{3}$

12. $\dfrac{2}{7}$ $\boxed{}$ $\dfrac{7}{8}$

13. $\dfrac{4}{5}$ $\boxed{}$ $\dfrac{3}{4}$

14. $\dfrac{1}{9}$ $\boxed{}$ $\dfrac{1}{5}$

15. $\dfrac{1}{6}$ $\boxed{}$ $\dfrac{2}{12}$

16. $\dfrac{2}{8}$ $\boxed{}$ $\dfrac{1}{4}$

Name _____ Skill: Less than, Greater than, Equal to

Compare the fractions. Write <, >, or = in each square to make a true math statement. The first one has been done for you.

1. $\frac{1}{6}$ $\boxed{<}$ $\frac{1}{4}$

2. $\frac{3}{5}$ $\square$ $\frac{1}{3}$

3. $\frac{3}{4}$ $\square$ $\frac{1}{2}$

4. $\frac{1}{2}$ $\square$ $\frac{6}{12}$

5. $\frac{4}{5}$ $\square$ $\frac{3}{10}$

6. $\frac{5}{9}$ $\square$ $\frac{1}{3}$

7. $\frac{6}{9}$ $\square$ $\frac{2}{3}$

8. $\frac{4}{5}$ $\square$ $\frac{3}{4}$

9. $\frac{1}{4}$ $\square$ $\frac{1}{7}$

10. $\frac{2}{4}$ $\square$ $\frac{1}{2}$

11. $\frac{2}{3}$ $\square$ $\frac{5}{6}$

12. $\frac{1}{6}$ $\square$ $\frac{1}{3}$

13. $\frac{2}{9}$ $\square$ $\frac{3}{4}$

14. $\frac{5}{7}$ $\square$ $\frac{3}{8}$

15. $\frac{4}{6}$ $\square$ $\frac{1}{2}$

16. $\frac{6}{8}$ $\square$ $\frac{3}{4}$

Read the paragraph carefully, then answer the questions. Write **NG** if there is not enough information given to answer the question.

Trenice sells insurance over the telephone. She makes many calls but does not always make a sale. This week she did pretty well! Monday she made 112 calls and 23 sales. Tuesday she made 94 calls and 31 sales. Wednesday Trenice made 67 calls and only 14 sales. She made 100 calls and 12 sales on Thursday. Friday was Trenice's day off so she went to the beach!

1. **How many calls did Trenice make on Wednesday and Friday?**

   _____

2. **How many sales did Trenice make this week?**

   _____

3. **How many calls did she make in all this week?**

   _____

4. **How many more calls did Trenice make than sales?**

   _____

5. **What did Trenice do on Saturday?**

   _____

6. **How many sales were made on Tuesday, Wednesday, and Thursday?**

   _____

7. **On Tuesday, how many more calls than sales were made?**

   _____

8. **How many more calls were made on Monday than on Thursday?**

   _____

Read the paragraph carefully, then answer the questions. Write **NG** if there is not enough information given to answer the question.

    David, Bobby, and Sam play on the Eagles baseball team. This season Bobby hit 9 home runs and 14 singles. David hit 10 home runs and 18 singles. Sam hit 3 home runs and 24 singles. The Eagles won 22 games and lost 8 games this season.

1. **What is the name of the boys' team?**

    _____

2. **What sport do the boys play?**

    _____

3. **How many home runs did all three boys hit this season?**

    _____

4. **Which boy hit the most singles?**

    _____

5. **How many games did the team play this season?**

    _____

6. **How many more singles than home runs did Sam hit?**

    _____

7. **How many singles did David and Bobby hit this season?**

    _____

8. **Which boy hit the least number of home runs?**

    _____

Name _____

Read the paragraph and chart carefully, then answer the questions. Write **NG** if there is not enough information given to answer the question.

Kasey kept track of the rainfall for her state for five months. Her findings are listed on the chart at the right.

April	14 inches
May	9 inches
June	8 inches
July	9 inches
August	12 inches

1. **How many months did Kasey keep a record of the rainfall?**

_____

2. **In which state does Kasey live?**

_____

3. **How much more rain fell in April than in August?**

_____

4. **Which two months had the same amount of rainfall?**

_____

5. **How much rain fell in April, May, and June?**

_____

6. **What was the total amount of rainfall for all five months?**

_____

7. **Which month had the lowest amount of rainfall?**

_____

8. **What was the difference in rainfall between April and June?**

_____

Answer Key

Name _____   Skill: Contractions

Rule

A **contraction** is two words joined together with one or more letters omitted and replaced by an apostrophe (').

I would = I'd
was not = wasn't

Rewrite each sentence, changing the underlined words to a contraction.

1. I am going to the movies this Friday.
   I'm going to the movies this Friday.
2. You are going to be late for school.
   You're going to be late for school.
3. He is my best friend.
   He's my best friend.
4. She would like some ice cream.
   She'd like some ice cream.
5. They are going to the beach.
   They're going to the beach.
6. The twins are not identical.
   The twins aren't identical.
7. The boys were not eating breakfast.
   The boys weren't eating breakfast.
8. We did not check the answers.
   We didn't check the answers.
9. We are having a party today.
   We're having a party today.
10. Let us begin the lesson.
    Let's begin the lesson.
11. You have given me plenty of reasons to study.
    You've given me plenty of reasons to study.
12. Joe should not touch the wet paint.
    Joe shouldn't touch the wet paint.

© Carson-Dellosa CD-3761   1

Name _____   Skill: Contractions

Rule

A **contraction** is two words joined together with one or more letters omitted and replaced by an apostrophe (').

I would = I'd
was not = wasn't

Rewrite each sentence, changing the underlined words to a contraction.

1. She will not run in the race today.
   She won't run in the race today.
2. They will try again tomorrow.
   They'll try again tomorrow.
3. The dogs are not barking.
   The dogs aren't barking.
4. I would not jump in the pool.
   I wouldn't jump in the pool.
5. The class has not gone to lunch.
   The class hasn't gone to lunch.
6. I did not think of that!
   I didn't think of that.
7. My television is not working.
   My television isn't working.
8. We have talked about this long enough.
   We've talked about this long enough.
9. They will sing in the chorus.
   They'll sing in the chorus.
10. We are happy to meet you.
    We're happy to meet you.
11. Who is your best friend?
    Who's your best friend?
12. Here is a map of the town.
    Here's a map of the town.

© Carson-Dellosa CD-3761   2

Name _____   Skill: Contractions

Rule

A **contraction** is two words joined together with one or more letters omitted and replaced by an apostrophe (').

I would = I'd
was not = wasn't

Rewrite each sentence, changing the underlined words to a contraction.

1. They are looking for you now.
   They're looking for you now.
2. Who would believe that story?
   Who'd believe that story?
3. I will be home by seven.
   I'll be home by seven.
4. They had better obey the rules!
   They'd better obey the rules.
5. I think she will like your artwork.
   I think she'll like your artwork.
6. I can not come to your party.
   I can't come to your party.
7. Jody did not know what was happening.
   Jody didn't know what was happening.
8. Later, you will clean your room.
   Later you'll clean your room.
9. I did not finish reading that book.
   I didn't finish reading that book.
10. I would like to have pasta for dinner.
    I'd like to have pasta for dinner.
11. Benny does not look happy.
    Benny doesn't look happy.
12. They have landed on the island.
    They've landed on the island.

© Carson-Dellosa CD-3761   3

Name _____   Skill: Word Usage

Rule

Its is a possessive pronoun. **It's** is a contraction for *it is* or *it has*.
Your is a possessive pronoun. **You're** is a contraction for *you are*.
It's a good idea to bring *your* coat. *You're* going to need *its* warmth.

Complete each sentence with the proper form of *its* or *it's*.

1. The puppy chased _____ its _____ tail.
2. _____ It's _____ a good day for a long walk.
3. We have been waiting and _____ it's _____ taking too long.
4. The table wobbles because _____ its _____ leg is broken.
5. _____ It's _____ the first time I have seen that.
6. The dog buried _____ its _____ bone.

Complete each sentence with the proper form of *your* or *you're*.

1. Is that _____ your _____ drawing?
2. _____ You're _____ a fine painter.
3. Where will you hang _____ your _____ picture?
4. I think _____ you're _____ nice.
5. _____ Your _____ mother is calling you.
6. _____ You're _____ the only one here.

Write four sentences using *its*, *it's*, *your*, and *you're*.

1. _____
2. _____ Answers will vary. _____
3. _____
4. _____

© Carson-Dellosa CD-3761   4

© Carson-Dellosa CD-3761   99

Answer Key

Name _____   Skill: Word Usage

Rule
Was and **were** are forms of the verb *be*. Use *was* after a singular subject or after the pronoun *I, he, she,* or *it*. Use *were* after a plural subject or after the pronoun *we, you,* or *they*.
He **was** glad they **were** coming to the game.

Complete each sentence with the proper form of *was* or *were*.

1. We _____ were _____ just about to leave.

2. Harrison and Mike _____ were _____ playing cards.

3. Kelsey _____ was _____ jumping rope.

4. The children _____ were _____ in the yard.

5. I _____ was _____ supposed to call you last night.

6. Marge _____ was _____ entering the contest.

7. Joe and Frank _____ were _____ playing in the rain.

8. They _____ were _____ jumping in the pile of leaves.

9. Cindy _____ was _____ baking some oatmeal cookies.

10. The raccoons _____ were _____ hiding in the bushes.

11. Jessie and Matt _____ were _____ looking for you.

12. The man _____ was _____ taking a nap.

Write four sentences using *was* and *were*.

1. _____
2. _____ Answers will vary. _____
3. _____
4. _____

5

Name _____   Skill: Word Usage

Rule
Good is an adjective; it describes a noun. **Well** is an adverb; it describes a verb.
You can also use *well* as an adjective to mean "healthy."
It's a *good* idea to study.   You scored *well* on the test.   He is a *well* man now.
adjective   *adverb*   *adjective (healthy)*

Complete each sentence with the proper form of *good* or *well*.

1. You sang _____ well _____ in the concert.

2. It was a _____ good _____ day for a hike.

3. I was ill, but now I feel _____ well _____ .

4. The floor is a _____ good _____ place to play with jacks.

5. He is a _____ good _____ looking man.

6. That meat was roasted _____ well _____ !

7. My puppy is _____ well _____ now, although he had been quite ill.

8. James always comes up with _____ good _____ ideas.

9. Casey is a _____ good _____ soccer player.

10. Our team will play _____ well _____ in the game.

11. The doctor gave him medicine to make him _____ well _____ .

12. That is a very _____ good _____ pie!

Write four sentences using *good* and *well*.

1. _____
2. _____ Answers will vary. _____
3. _____
4. _____

6

Name _____   Skill: Synonyms

Rule
Different words that have almost the same meaning are called **synonyms**.
Beautiful and *lovely* are synonyms.

Read the sentences and choices below. Circle the word that means almost the same thing as the word that is underlined in the sentence.

1. Patsy is <u>active</u> in the drama club. She acts and paints scenery.
   ability   (busy)   hard

2. The <u>youngster</u> wandered away from her mother.
   stubby   subject   (child)

3. Jerry gave lots of <u>affection</u> to his dog because they were best friends.
   (love)   blankets   unusual

4. The flower in the vase began to <u>wither</u> and turn brown.
   (dry)   grow   speck

5. Please do not <u>annoy</u> Chris. He has lots of homework to do.
   excuse   (bother)   ignore

6. Jonathan <u>placed</u> the books on the shelf.
   removed   lined   (put)

7. The <u>antique</u> book was dated 1866.
   modern   musty   (old)

8. The word the teacher used was <u>unfamiliar</u> to me.
   (unknown)   easy   collected

9. Mary wanted to get an "A" on the test, but she was <u>content</u> with a "B."
   admit   (satisfied)   upset

10. Justine knew that if she worked hard she would <u>achieve</u> success.
    attract   (reach)   struggle

7

Name _____   Skill: Synonyms

Rule
Different words that have almost the same meaning are called **synonyms**.
Beautiful and *lovely* are synonyms.

Read the sentences and choices below. Circle the word that means almost the same thing as the word that is underlined in the sentence.

1. It you <u>connect</u> the dots, they will make a picture!
   erase   draw   (join)

2. If you <u>intend</u> to finish painting before dinner, you had better hurry.
   (plan)   involve   dodge

3. I don't care for spinach. In fact, I <u>detest</u> it.
   enjoy   (hate)   humble

4. Can you <u>identify</u> the continents of the world?
   travel   color   (name)

5. Do you <u>like my</u> new shoes? Please give me your <u>honest</u> opinion.
   (truthful)   fringe   desired

6. The bird's nest was hidden in the <u>shrubs</u> outside the <u>window</u>.
   shuffles   dark   (bushes)

7. My <u>mind is</u> made up, so it will do no good to <u>quarrel</u> with me.
   (argue)   neglect   sniffle

8. Harvey shoveled a <u>mound</u> of snow off the sidewalk.
   (pile)   dribble   sod

9. The letter is so <u>skinny</u>, I can slide it right under the door.
   fat   (thin)   heavy

10. The soldier marched <u>onward</u> all day and night.
    quivering   loudly   (ahead)

8

Answer Key

Name _____   Skill: Synonyms

Rule
Different words that have almost the same meaning are called **synonyms**.
Beautiful and *lovely* are synonyms.

Read the sentences and choices below. Circle the word that means almost the same thing as the word that is underlined in the sentence.

1. Your mother said to call her right now. She said it is urgent!
   silly   willow   **important**

2. I want to sit near the window. Will you switch seats with me?
   swarm   **trade**   build

3. There was not one speck of dirt anywhere when Mom finished cleaning!
   spike   bucket   **spot**

4. It took me an hour, but I finally found the solution to that problem.
   answer   number   prime

5. The children picked up all the litter and threw it in the garbage can.
   shrimp   **trash**   extra

6. Delaney was confident she knew the answer to the question.
   certain   unsure   happy

7. It is not healthy to expose your skin to the hot sun for so long.
   bare   soften   cover

8. Students will display their projects in the art room next week.
   glimpse   **show**   feast

9. The house looked eerie sitting on top of the hill in those shadows.
   strange   bright   lower

10. The hikers began to ascend the mountain.
    climb   raise   draw

Name _____   Skill: Synonyms

Rule
Different words that have almost the same meaning are called **synonyms**.
Beautiful and *lovely* are synonyms.

Read the sentences and choices below. Circle the word that means almost the same thing as the word that is underlined in the sentence.

1. I have a job to do for my dad before I can play.
   chore   illness   lunch

2. We must alert the town that the flood is coming this way!
   drive   buckle   **warn**

3. Yolanda hurt her backbone when she fell off the horse.
   spine   ankle   shoulder

4. I have pushed for five minutes, but I can't budge this heavy box!
   open   paint   **move**

5. Larry challenged me to a race across the yard.
   spoiled   **dared**   hinted

6. The store was destroyed in the fire.
   ruined   built   festive

7. Melanie was furious when Pete insulted her.
   shy   **angry**   happy

8. The joyous sound of bells made me smile.
   sad   **happy**   golden

9. Jan got a nasty cut on her knee from the sharp rocks.
   bad   soft   cute

10. The hat looks ridiculous on my brother, so I made him remove it.
    fine   **silly**   great

Name _____   Skill: Antonyms

Rule
Words that have opposite meanings are called **antonyms**.
Before and *after* are antonyms.

Read the sentences and choices below. Circle the word that means the opposite of the word that is underlined in the sentence.

1. That bald baby has a shiny head.
   quiet   **hairy**   smiling

2. I don't play the piano well because I am just a beginner.
   child   **expert**   player

3. The party has just begun!
   arose   started   **ended**

4. The tea tasted bitter, so Macey made a face when she swallowed it.
   nasty   **sweet**   sour

5. The bold warrior marched fearlessly into battle.
   timid   brave   old

6. Sukie cautiously crossed the busy street.
   slowly   simply   **recklessly**

7. The cloudless sky was a brilliant blue today.
   cloudy   plain   beautiful

8. Ned will combine the sand and soil in one large bucket.
   dig   **separate**   lower

9. Jessie will complete her project by the end of the week.
   finish   **start**   fix

10. The man confessed that he was afraid of many things.
    admitted   sampled   **denied**

Name _____   Skill: Antonyms

Rule
Words that have opposite meanings are called **antonyms**.
Before and *after* are antonyms.

Read the sentences and choices below. Circle the word that means the opposite of the word that is underlined in the sentence.

1. We could hear the constant dripping of the faucet all night.
   irregular   unending   angry

2. Ice will thaw in the warmer weather.
   freeze   drip   melt

3. Dad had to crouch to see into the little doghouse.
   stand   crawl   squint

4. The woman proved she was innocent. She had not stolen the watch.
   honest   home   **guilty**

5. That was an excellent movie and I enjoyed it!
   terrible   wonderful   short

6. I will lend you a pencil so you can finish your homework.
   five   **borrow**   sharpen

7. The fire destroyed everything in its path.
   ruined   burned   **created**

8. The artist was modest about the many awards he had been given.
   boastful   shy   quiet

9. The mother was frantic when she lost her child in the crowd.
   helpful   **calm**   upset

10. Put a little water on this cloth so that it will be moist.
    damp   wet   **dry**

Answer Key

Name _____ Skill: Antonyms

Rule
Words that have opposite meanings are called **antonyms**.
Before and *after* are antonyms.

Read the sentences and choices below. Circle the word that means the opposite of the word that is underlined in the sentence.

1. We <u>rarely</u> go outside in this freezing weather.
   seldom   never   (often)

2. The hot, dry air was <u>cruel</u> to our skin!
   smart   mean   (kind)

3. Mr. Greene was <u>furious</u> when the dog dug up his flowers.
   (delighted)   angry   wild

4. The airplane began to <u>descend</u> from the sky toward the runway.
   sway   (rise)   dip

5. You were <u>fortunate</u> to find your <u>ring</u> after you lost it in the sand!
   lucky   (unlucky)   smart

6. The coach will <u>divide</u> the group into four teams.
   call   separate   (unite)

7. I get a lot of <u>pleasure</u> from reading good books.
   fun   (pain)   work

8. That roasted turkey looks <u>plump</u> and juicy!
   fat   golden   (slender)

9. The hungry boy <u>devoured</u> his dinner in less than a minute!
   cooked   (nibbled)   watched

10. There are <u>countless</u> stars in the night sky!
    amount   (few)   shiny

Name _____ Skill: Antonyms

Rule
Words that have opposite meanings are called **antonyms**.
Before and *after* are antonyms.

Read the sentences and choices below. Circle the word that means the opposite of the word that is underlined in the sentence.

1. On the whole team, John can <u>throw</u> the ball the <u>farthest</u>.
   fastest   (nearest)   best

2. Julia <u>hastily</u> hid the note under her book as the teacher walked by.
   (slowly)   angrily   quickly

3. Keaton <u>crumpled</u> up the paper and threw it away.
   picked   wrinkled   (smoothed)

4. The <u>raw meat</u> was not ready to be eaten.
   (cooked)   red   bitter

5. The <u>eldest</u> child was a girl and the rest were boys.
   prettiest   first   (youngest)

6. Tessie was full of <u>grief</u> when she lost her pet rabbit.
   (happiness)   sadness   sleepy

7. The cowboys <u>captured</u> the wild horses in the canyon.
   trapped   caught   (released)

8. The <u>entrance</u> to the school was near the gym.
   (exit)   door   fountain

9. It was so <u>foggy</u>, I could barely see to drive down the road.
   dark   misty   (clear)

10. At what <u>time</u> does the plane for Boston <u>depart</u>?
    (arrive)   leave   fly

Name _____ Skill: Homophones

Rule
Words that are pronounced the same way but have different meanings and spellings are called **homophones**.
Flower and *flour* are homophones.

Read the sentences and choices below. For each sentence, write the correct word in the blank.

1. If _____you're_____ ready, we can leave now.
   your   you're

2. Drive the tent _____stake_____ into the ground.
   stake   steak

3. I would like a _____piece_____ of pie, please.
   peace   piece

4. Does the puppy have muddy _____paws_____?
   pause   paws

5. Marcus could _____hear_____ the radio.
   hear   here

6. Did the _____brakes_____ stop the car in time?
   brakes   breaks

7. The school _____band_____ played in the parade.
   band   banned

8. I would like to _____dye_____ that shirt blue.
   die   dye

9. The two boys _____rowed_____ the boat across the lake.
   road   rowed   rode

10. What should Pearl _____wear_____ to the party?
    ware   wear

Name _____ Skill: Homophones

Rule
Words that are pronounced the same way but have different meanings and spellings are called **homophones**.
Flower and *flour* are homophones.

Read the sentences and choices below. Write the correct word in the blank.

1. Doris likes _____chili_____ on her hot dog.
   chilly   chili

2. Jimmy was _____bored_____ during the meeting.
   board   bored

3. We must _____flee_____ before the storm hits!
   flea   flee

4. Velma got her _____hair_____ cut quite short.
   hair   hare

5. What crops were _____grown_____ this year?
   grown   groan

6. Joe attached the sun catcher to the _____pane_____ in the window.
   pain   pane

7. My favorite dish is _____leek_____ and potato soup.
   leak   leek

8. The guide _____led_____ the group to safety.
   lead   led

9. Max took the _____reins_____ and guided the horse home.
   rains   reins   reigns

10. The green _____pear_____ is a tasty fruit.
    pair   pear   pare

Answer Key

Name _____   Skill: Homophones

Rule
Words that are pronounced the same way but have different meanings and spellings are called **homophones**.
Flower and *flour* are homophones.

Read the sentences and choices below. Write the correct word in the blank.

1. Has the _____ **mail** _____ been delivered yet?
   mail   male

2. There is _____ **no** _____ way I can do that for you.
   know   no

3. Calvin _____ **sent** _____ her a dozen roses.
   scent   sent

4. Which _____ **route** _____ will we take to Florida?
   route   root

5. Those silk flowers look so _____ **real** _____ .
   real   reel

6. Mother _____ **wrung** _____ out the wet clothes.
   wrung   rung

7. The flag was hanging on a tall _____ **pole** _____ .
   pole   poll

8. I do not like to eat the _____ **yolk** _____ of the egg.
   yoke   yolk

9. Sandy's family moved to _____ **Maine** _____ last year.
   main   Maine   mane

10. Those shoes gave me a blister on my _____ **heel** _____ .
    heal   heel   he'll

© Carson-Dellosa CD-3761   17

Name _____   Skill: Homophones

Rule
Words that are pronounced the same way but have different meanings and spellings are called **homophones**.
Flower and *flour* are homophones.

Read the sentences and choices below. Write the correct word in the blank.

1. How much does the cat _____ **weigh** _____ ?
   way   weigh

2. I like to _____ **vary** _____ the foods I eat each day.
   vary   very

3. We watched the _____ **tide** _____ leave the beach.
   tied   tide

4. Does an elephant have a long _____ **tail** _____ ?
   tail   tale

5. Martha had to _____ **shoo** _____ the dogs away.
   shoe   shoo

6. The _____ **scene** _____ in this play is very long.
   scene   seen

7. Jason broke three _____ **panes** _____ in the window.
   pains   panes

8. Did you _____ **peek** _____ at the presents?
   peek   peak

9. There are _____ **four** _____ books on the desk.
   for   fore   four

10. The _____ **ewe** _____ called for her lamb.
    ewe   you

© Carson-Dellosa CD-3761   18

Name _____   Skill: Vocabulary

Rule
Words that we understand and use in our daily language are called our **vocabulary**.

Complete each sentence by circling the word that means about the same thing as the underlined word or phrase.

1. A word that means a baby duck is ...
   chick   (duckling)   egg

2. To make longer is to ...
   decrease   supply   (extend)

3. A mask is a ...
   initial   (disguise)   lid

4. The word exhibit means ...
   (show)   enter   wander

5. Another word for educate is ...
   apply   school   (teach)

6. To exist is to ...
   leave   (live)   run

7. When you doze you are ...
   swimming   writing   (sleeping)

8. Another word for climate is ...
   (weather)   scale   land

9. Another word for sturdy is ...
   (rugged)   weak   tall

10. A person who is composed is ...
    (calm)   upset   tired

© Carson-Dellosa CD-3761   19

Name _____   Skill: Vocabulary

Rule
Words that we understand and use in our daily language are called our **vocabulary**.

Complete each sentence by circling the word that means about the same thing as the underlined word or phrase.

1. A word that means to join together is ...
   confuse   (connect)   blunder

2. To motion is to ...
   (gesture)   vanish   explain

3. A procession is a ...
   nation   role   (parade)

4. A word that means sad is ...
   (mournful)   plank   scarlet

5. Another word for area is ...
   meter   outfit   (region)

6. To find something is to ...
   lighten   (locate)   marvel

7. When you move forward you ...
   (progress)   fail   muffle

8. Another word for messy is ...
   (sloppy)   slippery   slant

9. A suggestion is a ...
   joke   demand   (proposal)

10. A person who watches is an ...
    inventor   (observer)   ostrich

© Carson-Dellosa CD-3761   20

© Carson-Dellosa CD-3761   103

Answer Key

Name _____ Skill: Vocabulary

Rule
Words that we understand and use in our daily language are called our **vocabulary**.

Complete each sentence by circling the word that means about the same thing as the underlined word or phrase.

1. A word that means to pause is ...
   impress   dare   (hesitate)

2. To amaze is to ...
   gulp   (dazzle)   launch

3. A cloth used at dinner is a ...
   (napkin)   plot   lodge

4. A word that means to answer a question is ...
   slither   contain   (respond)

5. The word seize means ...
   skim   process   (grab)

6. To pollute is to ...
   clean   (dirty)   bandage

7. When you feel prickly all over you ...
   (tingle)   waddle   stitch

8. Another word for tired is ...
   tread   (weary)   sturdy

9. A word that means to change is ...
   chase   count   (alter)

10. A person who is part of the family is a ...
    (relative)   inspector   numeral

© Carson-Dellosa CD-3761   21

Name _____ Skill: Vocabulary

Rule
Words that we understand and use in our daily language are called our **vocabulary**.

Complete each sentence by circling the word that means about the same thing as the underlined word or phrase..

1. A word that means faithful is ...
   rickety   honest   (loyal)

2. To get something back is to ...
   split   retreat   (recover)

3. To rest from work is to ...
   outwit   mingle   (relax)

4. The word recent means ...
   give   hate   (lately)

5. Another word for parcel is ...
   (package)   scrub   remark

6. To be modest is to be ...
   (humble)   boastful   sore

7. When you embroider you ...
   intend   (sew)   graze

8. A word that means huge is ...
   (massive)   skinny   social

9. A word that means crimson is ...
   (red)   instinct   kidnap

10. To make someone believe is to ...
    border   cloak   (convince)

© Carson-Dellosa CD-3761   22

Name _____ Skill: Context Clues

Rule
When you come to a word you don't know, use **context clues** (the meaning of the rest of the sentence or paragraph) to help you understand its meaning.

Use the context clues to figure out the meaning of each underlined word below. Circle the correct meaning.

1. After losing the lead in the second lap, Michael regained it in the third.
   (got back)   finished
   fell behind   stumbled

2. Betsy Ross was a patriot. She made the first flag for the United States.
   an artist   a traitor
   a chef   (a person loyal to a country)

3. Gazelle pulled a muscle in her thigh while running in the race.
   part of the hand   (part of the leg)
   part of the shoulder   a puppet

4. The artist wore a smock to protect her clothes from the paint.
   curtain   (a long, loose shirt)
   bag   a rubber band

5. This paper is due in one hour, so make all haste to get it done!
   erasers   careful
   (speed)   time

6. The watch had a luminous face. I could see it in the dark.
   round   dark
   (lighted)   purple

7. The police were in pursuit of the man who robbed the bank.
   (following)   anger
   video taping   running from

8. I must inform you that you are standing in the wrong line for those tickets.
   ask   supply
   (tell)   push

© Carson-Dellosa CD-3761   23

Name _____ Skill: Context Clues

Rule
When you come to a word you don't know, use **context clues** (the meaning of the rest of the sentence or paragraph) to help you understand its meaning.

Use the context clues to figure out the meaning of each underlined word below. Circle the correct meaning.

1. Acorns are plentiful in an oak forest.
   unusual   (abundant)
   large   rare

2. The lost pilot used the radio to make contact with the control tower.
   touch   direct
   (communicate)   lean on

3. My method of making a bed is to pull the cover over everything and walk away!
   (way or system)   quilt
   development   corner

4. The vase began to wobble and almost fell, but I caught it in time.
   (tip back and forth)   sing
   turn colors   shatter

5. The newspaper was old, yellow, and brittle, so we handled it very carefully.
   green   (easily broken)
   hard   soft

6. Mr. Thomas is a stamp collector. He keeps them all in a big album.
   person who eats out   a customer
   person who lies   (person who gathers things)

7. Vera shows great affection to her little sister because she loves her.
   (fond or tender feelings)   anger
   happiness   fear of

8. The hunters set out several snares to catch the rabbits.
   leashes   (traps)
   branches   carrots

© Carson-Dellosa CD-3761   24

Answer Key

Name _____   Skill: Context Clues

Rule
When you come to a word you don't know, use **context clues** (the meaning of the rest of the sentence or paragraph) to help you understand its meaning.

Use the context clues to figure out the meaning of each underlined word below.
Circle the correct meaning.

1. The child looked <u>bewildered</u> when she couldn't find her mother in the crowd.
   - excited
   - **(confused)**
   - lazy
   - dizzy

2. Does your purse <u>contain</u> a comb and a wallet?
   - **(hold)**
   - buy
   - use
   - unwrap

3. Jamie seemed very <u>earnest</u> about his plan.
   - bashful
   - untruthful
   - happy
   - **(serious)**

4. Don <u>challenged</u> Marcus to a race around the <u>track</u>.
   - invited
   - **(dared)**
   - threw
   - fought

5. After a good dinner and a warm bath, I feel <u>mellow</u>.
   - tense
   - upset
   - excited
   - **(relaxed)**

6. The hot water made my new shirt <u>shrink</u> and now it doesn't fit me.
   - get larger
   - discolor
   - **(get smaller)**
   - fade

7. I have a <u>request</u> of you. Please wipe your feet before coming in.
   - **(favor to ask)**
   - demand
   - statement
   - reply

8. Rain has been <u>scarce</u> lately, so the ground is dry.
   - heavy
   - plentiful
   - **(rare)**
   - messy

© Carson-Dellosa CD-3761   25

Name _____   Skill: Context Clues

Rule
When you come to a word you don't know, use **context clues** (the meaning of the rest of the sentence or paragraph) to help you understand its meaning.

Use the context clues to figure out the meaning of each underlined word below.
Circle the correct meaning.

1. I was very <u>tense</u> before I took that test.
   - wonderful
   - glad
   - **(nervous)**
   - angry

2. She smiled in <u>triumph</u> when she won the race!
   - sneer
   - **(victory)**
   - fear
   - jealousy

3. Dripping water is an <u>annoyance</u> when I am trying to study.
   - fun time
   - soothing sound
   - experience
   - **(bother)**

4. These two paintings are so much alike, I can't tell which is real and which is an <u>imitation</u>!
   - **(copy)**
   - western
   - unusual
   - connection

5. I really like the <u>flavor</u> of that new soda you bought. I drank the whole bottle!
   - price
   - color
   - advertisement
   - **(taste)**

6. I didn't <u>mean to neglect</u> you, but I have been too busy to see you lately.
   - **(ignore)**
   - play with
   - frighten
   - share

7. My shirt <u>shrunk</u> when it was washed in hot water.
   - stretched
   - froze
   - **(got smaller)**
   - disappeared

8. The howling puppies made such a <u>racket</u>, my neighbors called to complain.
   - playful
   - game
   - **(noise)**
   - paddle

© Carson-Dellosa CD-3761   26

Name _____   Skill: Context Clues

Rule
When you come to a word you don't know, use **context clues** (the meaning of the rest of the sentence or paragraph) to help you understand its meaning.

Use the context clues to figure out the meaning of each underlined word below.
Circle the correct meaning.

1. The ending of the play was <u>tragic</u>. The main <u>character</u> died.
   - too short
   - **(sad or serious)**
   - a wild, fun time
   - beginning

2. The <u>weary</u> hikers dragged themselves the <u>last</u> three miles of the long walk.
   - wiggly
   - **(tired)**
   - soggy
   - mean

3. The cup held a lot of water because of its large <u>volume</u>.
   - handle
   - color
   - saucer
   - **(amount of space)**

4. Devon looked <u>ridiculous</u> in that baby bunny costume.
   - **(silly)**
   - dramatic
   - respectful
   - serious

5. Those two boys look very <u>similar</u>. Are they twins or just brothers?
   - tall
   - different
   - **(alike)**
   - skinny

6. Have you <u>recovered</u> from that horrible cold?
   - sneezing
   - **(gotten better)**
   - warm
   - become worse

7. Her apology sounded <u>sincere</u>.
   - false
   - shameful
   - **(honest)**
   - funny

8. Nelson wants to be a <u>doctor</u> when he grows up.
   - nurse
   - actor
   - **(physician)**
   - man

© Carson-Dellosa CD-3761   27

Name _____   Skill: Fiction Comprehension

Rule
Comprehension questions test your ability to understand what you have read. When you understand a sentence or story, you **comprehend** it.

Read the story, then answer the questions about it.

Karen curled up on her bed with her favorite book. What a wonderful afternoon this would be! Karen had the house to herself for three hours, while her mom was visiting next door. She planned to eat snacks in her room, finish the book she was reading, and then watch television. As she lay on her bed, she thought about how quiet the house seemed. She could hear the clock ticking in the kitchen at the other end of the house. She could hear children playing outside across the street. Suddenly she heard something that didn't belong in her quiet world. Was someone at the back door? Karen's heart began to race as she heard the door creak open and then close. The next sound she heard was a familiar voice, "Karen, I'm home!"

1. **A good title for this story would be:**
   a. A Good Book
   b. Wasting the Day
   c. **(Home Alone in the Afternoon)**

2. **What three things did Karen plan to do that afternoon?** Karen planned to watch TV, finish a book, and eat snacks.

3. **What is a word that means "a harsh, squeaking sound"?**
   a. curled
   b. **(creak)**
   c. ticking

4. **Why was Karen home alone?** Her mom was visiting a neighbor.

5. **What words in the story tell you that Karen is scared?** Karen's heart began to race as she heard the door creak open.

6. **What would you do if you were Karen? Explain why.** Answers will vary.

© Carson-Dellosa CD-3761   28

Answer Key

Name _____   Skill: Fiction Comprehension

Rule
Comprehension questions test your ability to understand what you have read.
When you understand a sentence or story, you **comprehend** it.

Read the story, then answer the questions about it.

Carla pulled herself and her brother's sled up Blackmon's Hill. "What am I doing here?" she thought. "What if I get to the top and have to walk down?" The snowfall the day before had created perfect conditions for sledding. Kids of all ages and even parents were squealing as they went down the hill that leveled out in a wheat field that was now a soft, white blanket. Carla had never sledded anywhere but in the gentle slope of her backyard. What was it like to go so fast? What if she fell? She didn't want to look silly, but she was determined to conquer her fears. Then she saw Natalie sail by. She had baby-sat Natalie last summer! That did it! When Carla arrived at the top, she took a deep breath, pushed off, shut her eyes, and enjoyed the ride!

1. **A good title for this story would be:**
   a. Carla and Natalie
   b. Blackmon's Hill
   c. (Carla Conquers Her Fears)
2. **Why was Carla determined to sled the hill?** Carla wanted to conquer her fears.

3. **What is a word that means "conquer"?**
   a. forget
   b. (overcome)
   c. think about
4. **How does Carla feel about going down the hill?** Carla is afraid because she thinks she might fall.

5. **How old do you think Carla and Natalie are?**
   Answers will vary.

6. **What would you do if you were Carla? Explain.**
   Answers will vary.

© Carson-Dellosa CD-3761   29

Name _____   Skill: Fiction Comprehension

Rule
Comprehension questions test your ability to understand what you have read.
When you understand a sentence or story, you **comprehend** it.

Read the story, then answer the questions about it.

The plane's tires screeched as they hit the runway. R.J. leaned forward to watch as the passengers began to get off the plane. He had been waiting for this day for so long. His father was in the Navy and had been out on a submarine for a long time. It had been almost a year since R.J. had seen his dad. They wrote letters almost every week, but that wasn't the same as being together. The rush of passengers passed and still his father didn't come. R.J.'s excitement began to turn to disappointment as the last few passengers left the plane. His father wasn't there after all. But wait! What was this huge bear being pushed through the door? Suddenly his father's face peeked over its shoulder. Dad was home at last!

1. **A good title for this story would be:**
   a. The Airport
   b. R.J.'s Day
   c. (Dad Comes Home)
2. **Why was R.J. at the airport?** R.J. went to the airport to meet his father.

3. **What is a word that means "sadness"?**
   a. (disappointment)
   b. excitement
   c. peeked
4. **How long had it been since R.J. had seen his dad?** It had been almost a year since R.J. had seen his father.

5. **Why do you think his father was the last person off the plane?**
   R.J.'s father was the last person off the plane because he had to carry the big bear.

6. **Who would you most like to see getting off a plane? Explain why.**
   Answers will vary.

© Carson-Dellosa CD-3761   30

Name _____   Skill: Fiction Comprehension

Rule
Comprehension questions test your ability to understand what you have read.
When you understand a sentence or story, you **comprehend** it.

Read the story, then answer the questions about it.

Mrs. Jamison bent over her work on this warm spring day. She wanted to plant a vegetable garden to surprise her husband. He had not been well all winter, and fresh vegetables were his favorite food. Mr. Jamison had planted a garden every year for the forty-nine years they had been married. This year he was too sick to get outside. Mrs. Jamison was not in the best health herself, but she was determined to plant this garden. She took up the shovel and began the task of turning the soil. Suddenly she heard someone call her name. She looked up and saw ten-year-old David Lawson, her neighbor, standing in her yard with a shovel over his shoulder.

1. **A good title for this story would be:**
   a. Planting Seeds
   b. Gardening is Hard Work
   c. (Mrs. Jamison's Garden)
2. **What was Mrs. Jamison doing?** Mrs. Jamison was planting a garden for her husband.

3. **What is a word that means "to make up one's mind"?**
   a. (determine)
   b. health
   c. poorly
4. **How long had the Jamisons been married?** The Jamisons had been married for forty-nine years.

5. **What clues in the story let you know the Jamisons are older people?**
   The Jamisons have been married a long time.

6. **Why do you think David Lawson has his shovel? Explain.**
   Answers will vary.

© Carson-Dellosa CD-3761   31

Name _____   Skill: Fiction Comprehension

Rule
Comprehension questions test your ability to understand what you have read.
When you understand a sentence or story, you **comprehend** it.

Read the story, then answer the questions about it.

Yolanda smiled as she warmed the bottle of milk. Baby-sitting was her favorite thing to do, and this baby was a joy to care for because she was never fussy. Baby-sitting is pretty easy when you like children and Yolanda loved kids. She was very good at her job. Last year she took classes at the hospital that taught her how to care for babies and small children. She learned whom to call in an emergency and how to help a child that is choking. The classes made her more confident that she could handle almost any problem that might arise. She had a lot of fun watching the babies and playing with the children. Best of all, Yolanda was paid good money for a job she loved doing. What a great deal!

1. **A good title for this story would be:**
   a. (Yolanda's Job)
   b. Baby-sitting is No Fun
   c. Handling Babies
2. **What is Yolanda's job?** Yolanda is a baby-sitter.

3. **What is a word that means "an event that needs action or attention"?**
   a. hospital
   b. baby-sitting
   c. (emergency)
4. **Why does Yolanda feel so confident?** Yolanda is confident because she took a class at the hospital on how to care for children.

5. **Why does Yolanda feel so good about her work?** Yolanda feels good because she loves kids and gets paid for it.

6. **What would you like/not like about baby-sitting? Explain why.**
   Answers will vary.

© Carson-Dellosa CD-3761   32

Answer Key

Name _____ Skill: Nonfiction Comprehension

Rule
Comprehension questions test your ability to understand what you have read. When you understand a sentence or story, you **comprehend** it.

Read the story, then answer the questions about it.

People and animals eat plants. Did you know that some plants eat animals? The sundew plant is covered with tiny hairs and a sticky liquid. The liquid sparkles in the sun and catches the attention of, and then attracts an insect. As soon as the insect lands in the liquid, it becomes stuck. The hairs close over the insect and the plant digests, or eats it! There is another plant that can catch worms. The plant is a tiny fungus that spreads through the ground like thin threads. The threads have little loops growing on them that look like lassos. As a tiny worm crawls through the soil and passes through the loops, the loops tighten and the worm is caught. The fungus then digests the worm.

1. **A good title for this story would be:**
   a. Animals that Eat Plants
   b. (Plants that Eat Animals)
   c. Why We Live in Communities
2. **What makes insects come to the sundew plant?** Insects are attracted by the sparkling sticky liquid.

3. **What is a word that means "pull or draw closer"?**
   a. (attract)
   b. digest
   c. jump
4. **How does the fungus catch worms?** The fungus catches worms in its loops.

5. **What are the loops on the fungus compared to?** Loops on the fungus are compared to lassos.

6. **Which plant would you like to know more about? Why?**
   Answers will vary.

© Carson-Dellosa CD-3761   33

Name _____ Skill: Nonfiction Comprehension

Rule
Comprehension questions test your ability to understand what you have read. When you understand a sentence or story, you **comprehend** it.

Read the story, then answer the questions about it.

A lot of people have gardens in their yards. Gardens that are used to grow food are called *kitchen* or *vegetable gardens*. During World War II, these gardens were also called *victory gardens*. Some people like to grow plants that look pretty in their gardens. Many of these are *flower gardens* because they are filled with irises, roses, tulips, or other plants that flower. Plants that are raised to be researched, studied, or exhibited are kept in *botanical gardens*. Huge gardens that are kept beautiful year-round are often called *formal gardens*. There are gardens for every kind of plant you can think of, including cacti, trees, and pond plants. There are even *rock gardens*! These contain rocks and plants that are well-suited to grow among them.

1. **A good title for this story would be:**
   a. (All Types of Gardens)
   b. Vegetable Gardens Grow Food
   c. Formal Gardens are Pretty

2. **What did people call vegetable gardens during World War II?**
   Vegetable gardens were called victory gardens.

3. **What is a word that means "to study"?**
   a. botanical
   b. exhibit
   c. (research)

4. **Which kind of garden might you find at a castle or palace? Why?**
   Formal gardens or flower gardens are found at castles and palaces because they look nice.

5. **Which type of garden would you like to have? Why?**
   Answers will vary.

© Carson-Dellosa CD-3761   34

Name _____ Skill: Nonfiction Comprehension

Rule
Comprehension questions test your ability to understand what you have read. When you understand a sentence or story, you **comprehend** it.

Read the story, then answer the questions about it.

The words in the box make a riddle. This riddle describes something. Can you guess what it is? It's the letter "E"! Riddles have been used for thousands of years as a way to answer questions. Long ago, not many people could read or had the time to go to school. Knowledge was considered very valuable. When people were given a riddle instead of the answer, it helped them find the answer on their own. If they could not figure out the riddle, they would never know the answer to their question! Today, we use riddles more for fun than for knowledge, but they still make us think about things in new ways.

> The beginning of eternity,
> The end of time and space,
> The beginning of every end,
> The end of every place.

1. **A good title for this story would be:**
   a. The Answer
   b. Riddles are Not Funny
   c. (Riddles)
2. **How did people answer some questions years ago?** People answered questions using riddles.

3. **What is a word that means "smart"?**
   a. (wise)
   b. riddle
   c. answer
4. **What did people think was valuable?** People thought that knowledge was valuable.

5. **How do riddles help people?** Answers will vary.

6. **What is your favorite riddle? Why?**
   Answers will vary.

© Carson-Dellosa CD-3761   35

Name _____ Skill: Nonfiction Comprehension

Rule
Comprehension questions test your ability to understand what you have read. When you understand a sentence or story, you **comprehend** it.

Read the story, then answer the questions about it.

In early times, China was divided into several states. The rulers of some states built walls around their land for protection. About two thousand years ago, Shi Huangdi became the first emperor to bring all the Chinese states together. He decided to join the walls of the old states across the northern edge of China. Shi Huangdi's wall was 6 to 15 m (20 to 50 ft) tall and 4 to 12 m (13 to 40 ft) wide. Over the next 800 years, the wall was extended and used by other emperors. After that, it was pulled apart in many places and the stones were used to build homes. From 1368 to 1644, the wall was repaired and still stands in China today. The Great Wall of China is nearly 2,400 km (1,500 mi) long and can be seen from the moon!

1. **A good title for this story would be:**
   a. (The Great Wall of China)
   b. Emperor Shi Huangdi
   c. Walls
2. **What did the early Chinese people build to protect their states?**
   The Chinese people built walls to protect their states.

3. **What is a word that means "to make longer"?**
   a. repair
   b. (extend)
   c. emperor
4. **How tall is the Great Wall of China?**
   The wall is twenty to fifty feet tall.

5. **When the wall was torn down in places, how were the stones used?**
   The stones from the wall were used to build homes.

6. **Do you think the Great Wall still protects China? Explain.**
   Answers will vary.

© Carson-Dellosa CD-3761   36

Answer Key

Name _____ Skill: Nonfiction Comprehension

Rule
Comprehension questions test your ability to understand what you have read.
When you understand a sentence or story, you **comprehend** it.

Read the story, then answer the questions about it.

The pitch of a sound is how high or low the sound is. Birds generally make high-pitched sounds. The bang of a drum and a man's deep voice are low-pitched sounds. What makes these sounds different? Sound is made from vibrations, or back-and-forth movements. Vibrations travel outward in waves, like ripples on water. These waves carry the vibrations through the air to our ears. The faster something vibrates, the higher the pitch. The slower it vibrates, the lower the pitch. For example, stretch a rubber band between your fingers and then pluck it. The more it is stretched the faster the vibrations and the higher the pitch it makes. The looser it becomes, the slower the vibrations and the lower the pitch.

1. **A good title for this story would be:**
   a. What is Pitch?
   b. Playing the Rubber Band
   c. Vibrations Make Noise

2. **What two things named in the story have a low pitch?** The bang of a drum and a man's voice have a low pitch.

3. **What is a word that means "back-and-forth movement"?**
   a. pitch
   b. vibration
   c. sound

4. **What gives a noise a high pitch?** Faster vibrations give noise a high pitch.

5. **Name three sounds not in the story that have a low pitch:** Answers will vary.

6. **Do you prefer sounds with a high pitch or a low pitch? Explain.** Answers will vary.

© Carson-Dellosa CD-3761   37

Name _____ Skill: Letter Comprehension

Rule
Comprehension questions test your ability to understand what you have read.
When you understand a sentence or story, you **comprehend** it.

Read the letter below, then answer the questions about it.

April 14

Dear Christina,
I am so glad you came to visit my family for two weeks. Having you here was kind of like having a sister for a while! It was especially nice to have you here for my birthday. Thanks again for the neat game. I really like it! It was fun to go roller-skating together and I really liked having you come to school with me. Maybe I can come and visit your school this fall. My mom hasn't agreed yet, but she hasn't said "no" either. I know that you were disappointed when the pictures were not developed before you left, so I sent a copy of them to you with this letter. Do you like them? My favorite is the one where we are standing together at the skating rink. I think we look like twins, don't you? Write back soon. I miss you.
Your friend,
Marsha

1. **What is the purpose of this letter?** The purpose of this letter is to thank Christina for visiting.

2. **What is a word that means "to say yes"?**
   a. agree
   b. develop
   c. twins

3. **Name two things the girls did together during the visit:** The girls went roller-skating and went to school together.

4. **Which picture was Marsha's favorite?** Marsha's favorite picture shows the girls standing together at the skating rink.

5. **Who would you most like to visit? Explain why.** Answers will vary.

© Carson-Dellosa CD-3761   38

Name _____ Skill: Letter Comprehension

Rule
Comprehension questions test your ability to understand what you have read.
When you understand a sentence or story, you **comprehend** it.

Read the letter below, then answer the questions about it.

September 19

Dear Sir or Madam:
I am doing a math project at school, and I need your help. I really like your candy and enjoy eating the five colors in each bag (red, green, purple, yellow, and orange). I have purchased 15 bags of candy and will keep a chart showing how many candies of each color are in each bag (this is a "frequency distribution"). I predicted that there would be more red than any other color, because I usually find a lot of them in the bags I eat. I would like to know how you choose the colors that go into each bag. Do you have a taste test to see which color people like best? Is there supposed to be the same number of each color in every bag? Thank you for any information you can send to me.
A good customer,
Kevin

1. **What is the purpose of this letter?** The purpose of this letter is to get information about the different colors of the candy.

2. **What is a word that means "to guess what will happen"?**
   a. chart
   b. predict
   c. information

3. **Who is doing the "frequency distribution" project and for which class?** Kevin is doing the project for math class.

4. **How many candy colors are in each bag? What are they?** There are five colors in each bag: red, green, orange, purple, and yellow.

5. **What other question might Kevin ask this company? Explain why.** Answers will vary.

© Carson-Dellosa CD-3761   39

Name _____ Skill: Letter Comprehension

Rule
Comprehension questions test your ability to understand what you have read.
When you understand a sentence or story, you **comprehend** it.

Read the letter below, then answer the questions about it.

May 30

Dear Uncle Mark,
Here I am in Ireland at last! I have been here one week and am having a great time. We landed at Shannon Airport and spent the first night in the town of Bunratty. There is a castle in that town and we went to a feast, or huge dinner, just like the kings of long ago would have given. We drank mead, a drink made from honey, and ate lots of good foods. There were no forks back in the days of kings, so we ate most of the meal with our fingers. My favorite was the leek and potato soup which we drank straight from the bowls. On the way back to our hotel we were driving down a narrow road. As we came around a corner, we had to stop because a whole herd of cattle was coming down the road straight at us! I sure wish you were here to see this. I will write more soon.
Your niece,
Grace

1. **What is the purpose of this letter?** The purpose of this letter is to tell Grace's uncle about her trip to Ireland.

2. **What is a word that means "a drink made from honey"?**
   a. feast
   b. dagger
   c. mead

3. **Where is Grace?** Grace is on a trip to Ireland.

4. **What was unusual about the ride back to the hotel?** A herd of cattle was coming down the road.

5. **Which foreign country would you like to visit? Why?** Answers will vary.

© Carson-Dellosa CD-3761   40

Answer Key

Name _____   Skill: Nouns

Rule
A **common noun** is a word that names any person, place, or thing.
A **proper noun** names a specific person, place, or thing.
Common noun – girl
Proper noun – Susan

Underline all the nouns in each sentence. Identify the nouns as either common or proper by writing **C** under the common nouns and **P** under the proper nouns.

1. <u>Thomas Alva Edison</u> was a great <u>inventor</u>.
   P / C

2. We stayed in a <u>lodge</u> in <u>Minnesota</u>.
   C / P

3. The <u>books</u> are on the <u>shelves</u>.
   C / C

4. We saw that <u>advertisement</u> on <u>television</u>.
   C / C

5. The <u>bride</u> walked down the <u>aisle</u> of the <u>church</u>.
   C / C / C

6. The <u>soldier</u> fired the <u>cannon</u> at the <u>fort</u>.
   C / C / C

7. The <u>narrator</u>, <u>Mr. Oakley</u>, told the <u>story</u>.
   C / P / C

8. The <u>teacher</u> handed out a <u>packet</u> of <u>papers</u>.
   C / C / C

9. My <u>brother</u> gets into a <u>lot</u> of <u>mischief</u>.
   C / C / C

10. Was the <u>moth</u> eating <u>holes</u> in your <u>jacket</u>?
    C / C / C

11. The <u>pilot</u> said we are going to land in <u>Atlanta, Georgia</u> soon.
    C / P

12. <u>Mr. Burn's</u> <u>dog</u>, <u>Rusty</u>, won a <u>ribbon</u> at the <u>Middleville Dog Show</u>!
    P / C / P / C / P

© Carson-Dellosa CD-3761   41

Name _____   Skill: Nouns

Rule
A **common noun** is a word that names any person, place, or thing.
A **proper noun** names a specific person, place, or thing.
Common noun – girl
Proper noun – Susan

Underline all the nouns in each sentence. Identify the nouns as either common or proper by writing **C** under the common nouns and **P** under the proper nouns.

1. The <u>tourist</u> took a <u>lot</u> of <u>pictures</u> in <u>New York</u>.
   C / C / C / P

2. The <u>explorers</u> lit the <u>torch</u> as they entered the <u>cave</u>.
   C / C / C

3. The <u>solution</u> to the <u>puzzle</u> was hard!
   C / C

4. The <u>operator</u> dialed the <u>number</u> for my <u>friend</u> in <u>Oregon</u>.
   C / C / C / P

5. It took a <u>lot</u> of <u>lumber</u> to build the <u>house</u>.
   C / C / C

6. The <u>Tate Gallery</u> was filled with <u>art</u>.
   P / C

7. We had a <u>bowl</u> of <u>cereal</u> for <u>breakfast</u>.
   C / C / C

8. <u>Jose</u> is my <u>classmate</u> in <u>school</u>.
   P / C / C

9. The <u>ostrich</u> is a very large <u>bird</u>!
   C / C

10. The <u>hunter</u> set a <u>snare</u> for the <u>rabbit</u>.
    C / C / C

11. <u>Orion</u> is a <u>constellation</u> in the night <u>sky</u>.
    P / C / C

12. <u>Mr. Roberts</u> drives our <u>bus</u>.
    P / C

© Carson-Dellosa CD-3761   42

Name _____   Skill: Nouns

Rule
A **common noun** is a word that names any person, place, or thing.
A **proper noun** names a specific person, place, or thing.
Common noun – girl
Proper noun – Susan

Underline all the nouns in each sentence. Identify the nouns as either common or proper by writing **C** under the common nouns and **P** under the proper nouns.

1. The <u>scent</u> of <u>roses</u> drifted in through the open <u>window</u>.
   C / C / C

2. Our <u>neighbor</u>, <u>Mr. Marsh</u>, wore a <u>robe</u> over his <u>pajamas</u>.
   C / P / C / C

3. We picked delicious <u>fruit</u> at <u>Blake's Orchard</u>.
   C / P

4. <u>Jude</u> caught all those <u>fish</u> in that <u>lagoon</u>.
   P / C / C

5. <u>Ms. Greene</u>, an <u>architect</u>, drew <u>plans</u> for the new <u>house</u>.
   P / C / C / C

6. The <u>farmer</u> plowed the <u>cornfield</u> today.
   C / C

7. Turn off the <u>faucet</u> after washing your <u>hands</u>.
   C / C

8. <u>Maria</u> has a tiny <u>row</u> of <u>freckles</u> across her <u>cheeks</u>.
   P / C / C / C

9. Every <u>day</u> I rise at <u>daybreak</u>.
   C / C

10. I have <u>tickets</u> to see the <u>Miami Dolphins'</u> last <u>game</u> of the <u>year</u>.
    C / P / C / C

11. The <u>children</u> enjoy swimming in <u>Deidra's</u> <u>pool</u>.
    C / P / C

12. I saw a <u>flock</u> of <u>geese</u> flying south for the <u>winter</u>.
    C / C / C

© Carson-Dellosa CD-3761   43

Name _____   Skill: Nouns

Rule
A **common noun** is a word that names any person, place, or thing.
A **proper noun** names a specific person, place, or thing.
Common noun – girl
Proper noun – Susan

Underline all the nouns in each sentence. Identify the nouns as either common or proper by writing **C** under the common nouns and **P** under the proper nouns.

1. <u>Brian</u> poured his <u>coffee</u> into the <u>mug</u>.
   P / C / C

2. The <u>slope</u> was very steep!
   C

3. <u>Denise</u> sat on the <u>terrace</u> and enjoyed the <u>sun</u>.
   P / C / C

4. In <u>Alaska</u>, we heard <u>wolves</u> howling at the <u>moon</u>.
   P / C / C

5. The <u>nurse</u> put on her <u>uniform</u> for <u>work</u>.
   C / C / C

6. A small <u>sparrow</u> flew from the <u>nest</u>.
   C / C

7. <u>Mr. Parmenter</u>, the <u>librarian</u>, put the <u>books</u> back on the <u>shelves</u>.
   P / C / C / C

8. His <u>nephew</u>, <u>Jake</u>, is ten <u>years</u> old.
   C / P / C

9. The <u>sun</u> burned brightly on the <u>horizon</u>.
   C / C

10. I saw my <u>image</u> in the <u>mirror</u>.
    C / C

11. The <u>taxi</u> took us across <u>town</u> to <u>Bradford Avenue</u>.
    C / C / P

12. <u>Mrs. Pickford</u> moved from <u>Chicago</u> to <u>Dallas</u>.
    P / P / P

© Carson-Dellosa CD-3761   44

© Carson-Dellosa CD-3761   109

Answer Key

Name _____ Skill: Pronouns

Rule
A **pronoun** is a word that takes the place of a noun.
I, me, you, we, they, and *it* are pronouns.

Complete each sentence by choosing the correct pronoun and writing it in the blank.

1. _____ **I** _____ went to the dance last night.
   I   Me

2. _____ **You** _____ have dirty shoes.
   You   It

3. _____ **They** _____ won the championship.
   They   Me

4. Brian and Sue played together. _____ **They** _____ had fun.
   They   We

5. Susan opened the door and then _____ **she** _____ looked out.
   she   he

6. Wednesday was no fun because _____ **it** _____ rained all day.
   they   it

7. Mrs. Plum would like _____ **you** _____ to sit down now.
   you   he

8. Kaye's class put on a play for _____ **us** _____ .
   us   I

9. Roses are my favorite flower because _____ **they** _____ smell nice.
   they   he

10. Janice and I are eating. _____ **We** _____ will be finished soon.
    We   Us

© Carson-Dellosa CD-3761   45

Name _____ Skill: Pronouns

Rule
A **pronoun** is a word that takes the place of a noun.
I, me, you, we, they, and *it* are pronouns.

Complete each sentence by choosing the correct pronoun and writing it in the blank.

1. _____ **They** _____ are in the pool.
   They   I

2. _____ **He** _____ owns that old grey car.
   He   Me

3. _____ **She** _____ is a very nice girl.
   He   She

4. _____ **I** _____ must take this test myself.
   I   We

5. The book fell to the floor. _____ **It** _____ made a loud noise.
   It   He

6. Jane said that _____ **she** _____ forgot her jacket.
   she   we

7. Do _____ **you** _____ think it is a good picture?
   you   she

8. My parents are home. _____ **They** _____ couldn't come tonight.
   They   He

9. Ken and I are playing ball. _____ **We** _____ throw hard!
   We   They

10. _____ **She** _____ is my best friend.
    She   You

© Carson-Dellosa CD-3761   46

Name _____ Skill: Pronouns

Rule
A **pronoun** is a word that takes the place of a noun.
I, me, you, we, they, and *it* are pronouns.

Complete each sentence by choosing the correct pronoun and writing it in the blank.

1. Will you join _____ **me** _____ for lunch?
   you   me

2. _____ **I** _____ am going to school now.
   I   He

3. John stays late at work. _____ **He** _____ mops the floors.
   He   I

4. Jody's family went to Texas. _____ **They** _____ are on vacation.
   They   Us

5. Ned said _____ **he** _____ likes to play chess.
   you   he

6. Please pass the butter to _____ **me** _____ .
   I   me

7. That newspaper was edited by _____ **us** _____ .
   us   we

8. Emily wrote a poem. _____ **It** _____ is about trees.
   It   He

9. The water in the teakettle boiled. _____ **It** _____ was hot!
   You   It

10. John gave his jacket to Ellen. _____ **He** _____ was a gentleman!
    She   He

© Carson-Dellosa CD-3761   47

Name _____ Skill: Pronouns

Rule
A **pronoun** is a word that takes the place of a noun.
I, me, you, we, they, and *it* are pronouns.

Complete each sentence by choosing the correct pronoun and writing it in the blank.

1. _____ **They** _____ will be getting the mail soon.
   Me   They

2. _____ **I** _____ can't be late for school.
   I   It

3. Wayne and Ursula are laughing because _____ **they** _____ are happy.
   they   us

4. _____ **We** _____ can't decide where to have dinner.
   Us   We

5. Ashley is glad that _____ **she** _____ finished the test.
   she   us

6. Benjamin walks each day, but _____ **he** _____ never does at night.
   he   she

7. The plane is circling. _____ **It** _____ will land soon.
   She   It

8. The people rode on the bus. _____ **They** _____ were tired.
   They   She

9. _____ **I** _____ painted that picture on the wall.
   Me   I

10. _____ **We** _____ are going to bed now.
    We   I

© Carson-Dellosa CD-3761   48

© Carson-Dellosa CD-3761   110

Answer Key

Name _____   Skill: Action Verbs

> **Rule**
> An **action verb** shows action.
> *Jump*, *think*, and *sleep* are action verbs.

Underline the action verb(s) in each sentence.

1. Please <u>adjust</u> the television picture and <u>change</u> the channel.

2. Janice <u>combines</u> the milk and eggs before she <u>adds</u> the flour.

3. We <u>saluted</u> the flag and <u>began</u> the program.

4. Alyssa <u>stood</u> at the window and <u>watched</u> the rain.

5. Sally <u>requested</u> another seat on the plane.

6. We <u>trampled</u> over the carpet with muddy shoes.

7. That leaky fountain <u>squirted</u> water on his shirt.

8. Nancy <u>stitched</u> the hole in the pillow.

9. The old banana <u>rotted</u> in the hot sun.

10. Karen <u>predicts</u> that it will <u>snow</u> tomorrow.

11. Donald <u>paced</u> the floor nervously.

12. Cindy <u>fried</u> eggs while Tyrone <u>toasted</u> the bread.

13. Alice <u>chewed</u> the meat carefully.

14. Aunt Renee <u>washed</u> and <u>waxed</u> the floor today.

© Carson-Dellosa CD-3761   49

Name _____   Skill: Action Verbs

> **Rule**
> An **action verb** shows action.
> *Jump*, *think*, and *sleep* are action verbs.

Underline the action verb(s) in each sentence.

1. Bob <u>recalled</u> <u>seeing</u> the zebras at the zoo.

2. Thelma <u>directs</u> the school play each year.

3. The secretary <u>filed</u> the papers in the right drawer.

4. The eagle <u>soared</u> over the mountains.

5. Carol <u>hitched</u> the horse to the wagon.

6. We <u>endanger</u> alligators when we <u>hunt</u> them.

7. Sue <u>unclasped</u> her purse and <u>removed</u> her wallet.

8. Our team <u>defeated</u> your team last year.

9. R.J. <u>launched</u> the toy rocket.

10. Did the hail <u>damage</u> the car during the storm?

11. The peaches <u>ripened</u> in the warm sunshine.

12. My pencil <u>fell</u> off the desk and <u>rolled</u> across the floor.

13. The notebook <u>caught</u> my sleeve and <u>tore</u> it.

14. I <u>packed</u> my suitcase and <u>carried</u> it to the door.

© Carson-Dellosa CD-3761   50

Name _____   Skill: Action Verbs

> **Rule**
> An **action verb** shows action.
> *Jump*, *think*, and *sleep* are action verbs.

Underline the action verb(s) in each sentence.

1. In winter, some birds <u>migrate</u> to warmer places.

2. Jamie <u>scowled</u> when she <u>lost</u> the contest.

3. We <u>proceeded</u> with the plans for Kim's surprise party.

4. We <u>smothered</u> the fire before we <u>left</u> camp.

5. Patrick <u>scraped</u> his knee when he <u>fell</u>.

6. Our choir <u>traveled</u> to London and <u>sang</u> in Hyde Park last spring.

7. Dad <u>located</u> Water Street on the map.

8. Candace <u>muttered</u> her lines in the play, so no one <u>heard</u> them.

9. They <u>plunged</u> into the water to <u>cool</u> themselves.

10. The woman <u>stood</u> and <u>prepared</u> to <u>leave</u> the meeting.

11. Jim <u>settled</u> into bed and <u>turned</u> out the light.

12. Debbie <u>rode</u> her bicycle to Martha's house.

13. Steve <u>peeled</u> the potatoes and <u>cooked</u> them in the pot.

14. Jody <u>finished</u> her homework and then <u>called</u> Judy.

© Carson-Dellosa CD-3761   51

Name _____   Skill: Linking Verbs

> **Rule**
> A **linking verb** does not show action but shows a state of being. It connects the subject of a sentence to a word(s) that describes or renames the subject. Linking verbs are usually forms of *be*, such as *am, is, are, was,* and *were.*
> The cow **was** black and white.

1. Mary <u>was</u> happy when so many people attended her dance recital.

2. Kelsey <u>is</u> sorry she missed the party.

3. Mysteries <u>are</u> my favorite type of book!

4. Today <u>is</u> January third.

5. We <u>were</u> pleased to see our team win the game.

6. Kay <u>was</u> amused when Ken told jokes.

7. I am anxious <u>to</u> finish my homework before dinner.

8. Mr. Alton <u>was</u> quiet during the concert.

9. The kitten <u>was</u> frightened when the dog barked.

10. The two little boys <u>were</u> happy to find the large mud puddle.

11. Nathan and I <u>were</u> calm during the storm, but the others <u>were</u> upset.

12. My favorite color <u>is</u> blue.

13. We <u>are</u> tired and want to go to bed.

14. That present <u>is</u> the one I brought to the party.

© Carson-Dellosa CD-3761   52

Answer Key

Name _____ Skill: Adjectives

Rule
An **adjective** is a word that describes a noun or a pronoun.
Playful is an adjective that could describe the noun, *puppy*.

Complete each sentence by choosing an adjective from the word box and writing it in the blank. Use each word only once.

1. The _____ average _____ grade on the test was a "B."

2. Mother made some _____ bitter _____ tea for my cold.

3. The new _____ copper _____ penny was shiny and bright.

4. It was funny to see a _____ bald _____ man at the barbershop.

5. The _____ skillful _____ artist drew our portrait.

6. Grandma's _____ antique _____ chair was sold for a lot of money.

7. There were _____ twenty-one _____ floats in the parade.

8. The actor gave an _____ incredible _____ performance!

9. Those _____ violet _____ flowers are blooming in my garden.

10. The _____ weary _____ traveler just wanted to go to sleep.

11. Keisha and I have _____ opposite _____ views on which game to play.

12. That _____ comfortable _____ quilt kept me warm all night.

WORD BOX			
weary	average	incredible	antique
copper	twenty-one	bitter	bald
skillful	opposite	comfortable	violet

© Carson-Dellosa CD-3761   53

Name _____ Skill: Adjectives

Rule
An **adjective** is a word that describes a noun or a pronoun.
Playful is an adjective that could describe the noun, *puppy*.

Complete each sentence by choosing an adjective from the word box and writing it in the blank. Use each word only once.

1. Lyle had _____ vanilla _____ ice cream for dessert.

2. The _____ blue-eyed _____ doll is my favorite.

3. We had an _____ unexpected _____ visitor in our class today.

4. The _____ bold _____ child wasn't afraid of failure.

5. Mother gave me a _____ pearl _____ ring for my birthday.

6. The _____ foggy _____ weather made it difficult to drive.

7. Judd likes to listen to _____ classical _____ music.

8. That _____ unfriendly _____ family won't talk to their neighbors.

9. The _____ bony _____ fish was difficult to eat.

10. We had _____ garlic _____ bread with the spaghetti.

11. I like to have a _____ plump _____ pillow on my bed.

12. The _____ glossy _____ lipstick was too shiny.

WORD BOX			
unexpected	vanilla	foggy	classical
bony	pearl	bold	unfriendly
plump	glossy	garlic	blue-eyed

© Carson-Dellosa CD-3761   54

Name _____ Skill: Adjectives

Rule
An **adjective** is a word that describes a noun or a pronoun.
Playful is an adjective that could describe the noun, *puppy*.

Complete each sentence by choosing an adjective from the word box and writing it in the blank. Use each word only once.

1. The _____ generous _____ man gave a lot of money to charity.

2. That _____ ridiculous _____ hat should be on a clown!

3. There were _____ numerous _____ colors from which to choose.

4. His _____ unkind _____ words hurt my feelings.

5. That _____ skinny _____ dog looks very hungry.

6. The _____ restless _____ children wanted to go outside and play.

7. The _____ frozen _____ meat was not ready to be cooked.

8. Felicia is the _____ eldest _____ of the six children.

9. I had an _____ eerie _____ feeling I was being watched.

10. Buy _____ sturdy _____ boots for climbing mountains.

11. We spent six _____ glorious _____ days in Hawaii.

12. That _____ rotten _____ apple should be thrown away.

WORD BOX			
unkind	restless	sturdy	eerie
generous	numerous	ridiculous	frozen
rotten	eldest	glorious	skinny

© Carson-Dellosa CD-3761   55

Name _____ Skill: Adjectives

Rule
An **adjective** is a word that describes a noun or a pronoun.
Playful is an adjective that could describe the noun, *puppy*.

Complete each sentence by choosing an adjective from the word box and writing it in the blank. Use each word only once.

1. The _____ wealthy _____ man bought a palace in France.

2. Caitlin wore a _____ fluffy _____ fur to the party.

3. That _____ cruel _____ person was mean to the animals.

4. I've never seen anything like this. What an _____ original _____ painting!

5. I had a _____ tremendous _____ headache last night.

6. The _____ prickly _____ cactus caught my jacket as I passed.

7. The _____ raw _____ hamburger could not be eaten.

8. Those are _____ sensible _____ shoes for such a long walk.

9. Fred was the _____ eighth _____ person in line.

10. The _____ stale _____ bread was too hard to eat.

11. The _____ sloppy _____ woman made a mess in the kitchen.

12. I like _____ raspberry _____ jelly on my toast.

WORD BOX			
cruel	tremendous	wealthy	sloppy
stale	raw	sensible	fake
raspberry	eighth	prickly	original

© Carson-Dellosa CD-3761   56

Answer Key

Name _____ Skill: Adverbs

Rule

An **adverb** is a word that describes a verb or adjective.
Adverbs answer the questions *where?, when?, how?,* or *to what extent?*
Please speak *quietly* in the library. *Quietly* answers the question,
"How should I speak in the library?"

Complete each sentence by choosing an adverb from the word box and writing it in the blank. Use each word only once.

1. The ship signaled _____ **frantically** _____ for help.
2. We walked _____ **hurriedly** _____ across the busy street.
3. Jessie will run _____ **ahead** _____ and warn the others.
4. Brad _____ **secretly** _____ hid the map in the bottom of a box.
5. The girl spoke _____ **sweetly** _____ to her father.
6. I am glad that you are feeling _____ **better** _____ .
7. How many pencils do I have _____ **altogether** _____ ?
8. Jacob dived _____ **fearlessly** _____ into the water.
9. They celebrated _____ **joyously** _____ when they won!
10. The watch was _____ **very** _____ expensive.
11. Mother promised that we will be leaving _____ **soon** _____ .
12. We worked _____ **hard** _____ all afternoon.

WORD BOX			
altogether	secretly	ahead	hard
soon	hurriedly	fearlessly	joyously
frantically	better	sweetly	very

© Carson-Dellosa CD-3761   57

Name _____ Skill: Adverbs

Rule

An **adverb** is a word that describes a verb or adjective.
Adverbs answer the questions *where?, when?, how?,* or *to what extent?*
Please speak *quietly* in the library. *Quietly* answers the question,
"How should I speak in the library?"

Complete each sentence by choosing an adverb from the word box and writing it in the blank. Use each word only once.

1. Howard walked _____ **bravely** _____ into the dark room.
2. We talked _____ **excitedly** _____ about our plans for the party.
3. Maggie _____ **gently** _____ patted the hurt dog.
4. I will go to the zoo _____ **tomorrow** _____ . I don't want to go today.
5. May we go to the movies _____ **now** _____ ?
6. The runners raced _____ **swiftly** _____ around the track.
7. The thunder seemed to go on booming _____ **endlessly** _____ .
8. T. J. threw the darts _____ **wildly** _____ at the board.
9. Please put the smelly trash can _____ **outside** _____ .
10. I know I left that book _____ **somewhere** _____ .
11. Salvator danced _____ **gracefully** _____ around the room.
12. The mountain climbers are coming _____ **down** _____ .

WORD BOX			
bravely	gently	gracefully	wildly
somewhere	endlessly	swiftly	tomorrow
now	excitedly	down	outside

© Carson-Dellosa CD-3761   58

Name _____ Skill: Adverbs

Rule

An **adverb** is a word that describes a verb or adjective.
Adverbs answer the questions *where?, when?, how?,* or *to what extent?*
Please speak *quietly* in the library. *Quietly* answers the question,
"How should I speak in the library?"

Complete each sentence by choosing an adverb from the word box and writing it in the blank. Use each word only once.

1. Please put all your books _____ **away** _____ .
2. Bob wandered _____ **aimlessly** _____ through the woods.
3. Hillary _____ **carefully** _____ traced the drawing.
4. Halley looked _____ **lovingly** _____ at her brother.
5. Tara tiptoed _____ **softly** _____ across the floor.
6. We should meet right _____ **here** _____ after lunch.
7. I got an "A" on my test _____ **yesterday** _____ !
8. I have _____ **often** _____ wished for a million dollars.
9. We could _____ **faintly** _____ hear the train coming our way.
10. Norman _____ **silently** _____ read the book.
11. Jason is _____ **almost** _____ finished with dinner.
12. I need to feed all my pets _____ **daily** _____ .

WORD BOX			
here	away	daily	faintly
carefully	softly	aimlessly	lovingly
often	silently	yesterday	almost

© Carson-Dellosa CD-3761   59

Name _____ Skill: Adverbs

Rule

An **adverb** is a word that describes a verb or adjective.
Adverbs answer the questions *where?, when?, how?,* or *to what extent?*
Please speak *quietly* in the library. *Quietly* answers the question,
"How should I speak in the library?"

Complete each sentence by choosing an adverb from the word box and writing it in the blank. Use each word only once.

1. We sat _____ **lazily** _____ in the sun and snoozed.
2. Corey threw the ball _____ **high** _____ into the air.
3. The children clattered _____ **noisily** _____ down the stairs.
4. I could _____ **never** _____ eat all that food!
5. Ginger always speaks _____ **nicely** _____ to her friends.
6. Everyone looked _____ **upward** _____ as the eagle flew over.
7. The day dragged on _____ **endlessly** _____ .
8. Sleepy Sandra looked _____ **longingly** _____ at her bed.
9. Carla shook her fist _____ **angrily** _____ .
10. I must get to bed early _____ **tonight** _____ !
11. Janice and Philip put the model train _____ **together** _____ .
12. The twins _____ **anxiously** _____ waited for the plane to land.

WORD BOX			
longingly	noisily	tonight	never
anxiously	lazily	upward	together
high	endlessly	angrily	nicely

© Carson-Dellosa CD-3761   60

© Carson-Dellosa CD-3761   113

Answer Key

Panel 1 (page 61)

Name _____   Skill: Subject

Rule
The **simple subject** is a noun or pronoun that tells whom or what the sentence is about.
The **complete subject** includes the simple subject and all the words that tell more about it.
The white cat slept on the pillow.
The simple subject is *cat* and the complete subject is *The white cat.*

Underline the complete subject of each sentence. Circle the simple subject.

1. My green and yellow (ball) bounced across the lawn.
2. The (girl) with blue ribbons in her hair is my sister.
3. The large (lion) roared at the tiny mouse.
4. (We) ate at that restaurant last week.
5. The (man) with the hat is my father.
6. His older (sister) went to Mexico.
7. The (puppy) with the red collar is running toward the lake.
8. The little green (lizard) jumped from leaf to leaf.
9. (School) starts next week!
10. (Mr. Martinez) is a great coach.
11. A (salesman) knocked on the front door.
12. That (haircut) looks very nice on you.

Write your own subject for each sentence.

1. Answers will vary. _____ swam all day.
2. _____ drank iced tea.
3. _____ said she was tired.
4. _____ looked over her shoulder.

© Carson-Dellosa CD-3761   61

Panel 2 (page 62)

Name _____   Skill: Subject

Rule
The **simple subject** is a noun or pronoun that tells whom or what the sentence is about.
The **complete subject** includes the simple subject and all the words that tell more about it.
The white cat slept on the pillow.
The simple subject is *cat* and the complete subject is *The white cat.*

Underline the complete subject of each sentence. Circle the simple subject.

1. Uncle (Brian) is mailing the book to me.
2. Our (class) will read six books this year.
3. (Turkey) with stuffing is my favorite meal.
4. (Harmon) has to take medicine for his cold.
5. The (telephone) was ringing.
6. (Marissa) left a message on the answering machine.
7. The three-year-old (child) was hiding under the table.
8. Chrissy's (dress) with the yellow flowers was torn on the chair.
9. That brown (clock) is ticking too loudly!
10. The red and orange (sunset) was lovely.
11. Those two (babies) are twins.
12. The (Grand Canyon) is beautiful.

Write your own subject for each sentence.

1. Answers will vary. _____ ran along the beach.
2. _____ ate too much.
3. _____ will take a nap.
4. _____ watched television.

© Carson-Dellosa CD-3761   62

Panel 3 (page 63)

Name _____   Skill: Subject

Rule
The **simple subject** is a noun or pronoun that tells whom or what the sentence is about.
The **complete subject** includes the simple subject and all the words that tell more about it.
The white cat slept on the pillow.
The simple subject is *cat* and the complete subject is *The white cat.*

Underline the complete subject of each sentence. Circle the simple subject.

1. The (window) in the hallway cracked during the storm.
2. (Jason) hid under his bed.
3. The (hat) with the red feather looks nice on you.
4. The fuzzy (kittens) were sitting on the couch.
5. My (fingernails) are getting long!
6. The (newspaper) was delivered early this morning.
7. The (Spanish Club) is taking a trip to Mexico City.
8. Marsha's (hand) is not as big as mine.
9. The elegant (hotel) had brass lamps in the lobby.
10. (I) would like to go now.
11. My (neighbor), Mr. Green, took his son to a ball game.
12. The screaming (fans) enjoyed the game.

Write your own subject for each sentence.

1. Answers will vary. _____ wrote a book.
2. _____ mowed the lawn.
3. _____ has seven pets.
4. _____ turned on the light.

© Carson-Dellosa CD-3761   63

Panel 4 (page 64)

Name _____   Skill: Subject

Rule
The **simple subject** is a noun or pronoun that tells whom or what the sentence is about.
The **complete subject** includes the simple subject and all the words that tell more about it.
The white cat slept on the pillow.
The simple subject is *cat* and the complete subject is *The white cat.*

Underline the complete subject of each sentence. Circle the simple subject.

1. The oldest (person) in the room was ninety-four.
2. That old (letter) was written over one hundred years ago!
3. (Pamela) took her mother shopping.
4. The prince's (horse) reared and kicked its feet.
5. The (post office) is closed on Sunday.
6. My hungry (brother) ate half my ice cream.
7. The green (flag) belongs to my team.
8. (Alphonse) raced around the room.
9. The huge diamond (ring) sparkled in the sunlight.
10. Snow-capped (mountains) are beautiful.
11. The sleepy (boy) yawned.
12. The green (goggles) belong to Amy.

Write your own subject for each sentence.

1. Answers will vary. _____ sat down on the step.
2. _____ looked at the photo.
3. _____ understood.
4. _____ cried all night.

© Carson-Dellosa CD-3761   64

Answer Key

Name _____   Skill: Predicate

Rule
The **simple predicate** is a verb that tells what the subject did or what was done to the subject.
The **complete predicate** includes the verb and all the words that tell more about it.
The white cat slept on the pillow.
The simple predicate is *slept* and the complete predicate is *slept on the pillow.*

Underline the complete predicate of each sentence. Circle the simple predicate.

1. The adventure (began) early that morning.
2. Tonya and Tony (rowed) the boat to shore.
3. The wind (blew) through the trees.
4. They (live) in the house on the hill.
5. The horses and cattle (came) back to the barn at night.
6. Mr. Weiss (cracks) the ice for our sodas.
7. That restaurant (serves) lobster.
8. Donna and Fred (cooked) a delicious dinner.
9. The tree (grew) about three feet each year.
10. Roger (watches) television with us.
11. Michael (plays) baseball with that team.

Write your own predicate for each sentence.

1. Patsy and Tom __Answers will vary._____ .
2. The brown book _____ .
3. The computer near the window _____ .
4. Paula _____ .

© Carson-Dellosa CD-3761   65

Name _____   Skill: Predicate

Rule
The **simple predicate** is a verb that tells what the subject did or what was done to the subject.
The **complete predicate** includes the verb and all the words that tell more about it.
The white cat slept on the pillow.
The simple predicate is *slept* and the complete predicate is *slept on the pillow.*

Underline the complete predicate of each sentence. Circle the simple predicate.

1. Bess (danced) in the school play.
2. We (went) to the mall after the library.
3. California (is) a state on the west coast.
4. The weather (began) to turn cool.
5. It (rained) for hours yesterday!
6. Opal (made) a painting for her mom.
7. Snow (fell) for six hours.
8. Seven students (were) in the spelling bee.
9. The tractor (made) a loud noise.
10. We (served) ice cream and cake at the party.
11. The children (raced) to the end of the block.

Write your own predicate for each sentence.

1. The big shoes __Answers will vary._____ .
2. My pet _____ .
3. That field _____ .
4. The largest building _____ .

© Carson-Dellosa CD-3761   66

Name _____   Skill: Predicate

Rule
The **simple predicate** is a verb that tells what the subject did or what was done to the subject.
The **complete predicate** includes the verb and all the words that tell more about it.
The white cat slept on the pillow.
The simple predicate is *slept* and the complete predicate is *slept on the pillow.*

Underline the complete predicate of each sentence. Circle the simple predicate.

1. Aunt Tina (sent) a beautiful card for my birthday.
2. My dad (likes) to read books about history.
3. Dorothy (drives) a red truck.
4. Those men (cut) down the tall pine tree.
5. We (ate) popcorn during the movie.
6. The lemonade (tasted) sweet.
7. Judy (saw) exactly what happened.
8. Penny (rode) the black horse.
9. An old car (rattled) down the street.
10. Our team (won) the trophy!
11. The squirrel (hid) the acorn under the tree.

Write your own predicate for each sentence.

1. This crayon __Answers will vary._____ .
2. I _____ .
3. The red sweater _____ .
4. Hot sand _____ .

© Carson-Dellosa CD-3761   67

Name _____   Skill: Predicate

Rule
The **simple predicate** is a verb that tells what the subject did or what was done to the subject.
The **complete predicate** includes the verb and all the words that tell more about it.
The white cat slept on the pillow.
The simple predicate is *slept* and the complete predicate is *slept on the pillow.*

Underline the complete predicate of each sentence. Circle the simple predicate.

1. Red and blue fireworks (burst) in the night sky.
2. The lamp (fell) off the table.
3. Many leaves on the trees (turned) red this week.
4. The brisk fall days (felt) chilly.
5. Jerry and Vernon (went) home.
6. We (changed) the channel at nine o'clock.
7. Alex (wants) another cookie.
8. The mosquito (bit) me on the nose.
9. Abigail and her sister (told) that story to the children.
10. Mike (put) the onions in the soup.
11. Joey and David (went) fishing.

Write your own predicate for each sentence.

1. The telephone __Answers will vary._____ .
2. Your jacket _____ .
3. Fran's grandmother _____ .
4. The baby in the stroller _____ .

© Carson-Dellosa CD-3761   68

Answer Key

Name _____   Skill: Fragments

Rule

A **sentence** is a group of words that expresses a complete thought.
A **fragment** is an incomplete sentence because it does not express a complete thought.
Fragments: *Anna and Beth.* (missing a predicate that tells what happened)
              Went swimming. (missing a subject that tells who)
Sentence: *Anna and Beth went swimming.*

Write **S** if the words below form a sentence and **F** if they are a fragment.

F 1. Into the tall grass.

S 2. Janice ate the cake.

F 3. The boy in the dark blue suit.

F 4. After we eat.

S 5. The elephants blew water out of their trunks!

F 6. Never went there again.

F 7. The beautiful lake at the bottom of the mountain.

S 8. Candace ate corn.

S 9. The small bug crawled into the crack.

F 10. Under the leaves we raked yesterday.

S 11. Donald swam all day.

S 12. Carol is calling us.

Add words to make each phrase a sentence.

1. Frances gathered __Answers will vary.__ .

2. _____ clothes on the line.

3. A low rumble _____ .

4. _____ disappeared!

© Carson-Dellosa CD-3761   69

Name _____   Skill: Fragments

Rule

A **sentence** is a group of words that expresses a complete thought.
A **fragment** is an incomplete sentence because it does not express a complete thought.
Fragments: *Anna and Beth.* (missing a predicate that tells what happened)
              Went swimming. (missing a subject that tells who)
Sentence: *Anna and Beth went swimming.*

Write **S** if the words below form a sentence and **F** if they are a fragment.

F 1. Rang loudly and woke all of us!

F 2. Down the dark tunnel and into a large cave.

F 3. Pete and his cousin, Elmo.

S 4. We will play a game after dinner.

S 5. You may come along with us.

S 6. The darts hit the board.

F 7. Around the corner and over the bridge.

S 8. That is my house.

S 9. Frank ate the beans.

F 10. A hot dog and some potato chips.

S 11. She is a shy girl.

F 12. The states of Texas, Michigan, and New York.

Add words to make each phrase a sentence.

1. After the rainstorm we __Answers will vary.__ .

2. _____ munching on apples.

3. Kelly _____ .

4. _____ over our heads.

© Carson-Dellosa CD-3761   70

Name _____   Skill: Capitalization

Rule

Remember to use **capital letters** for:
  • the first word in a sentence • the pronoun "I"
  • proper nouns • important words in book and movie titles

Each sentence has one or more capitalization mistakes. Write each sentence correctly on the line below it.

1. jeff plays the piano every thursday afternoon. __Jeff plays the piano every Thursday afternoon.__

2. this october, we will take a trip to williamsburg, virginia. __This October, we will take a trip to Williamsburg, Virginia.__

3. i told mrs. potter that her cat, fluffy, was on the roof again. __I told Mrs. Potter that her cat, Fluffy, was on the roof again.__

4. next year, i will be in the fifth grade at carver elementary school. __Next year, I will be in the fifth grade at Carver Elementary School.__

5. buffalo once lived in many parts of north america. __Buffalo once lived in many parts of North America.__

6. my aunt linda visited friends in france and italy. __My Aunt Linda visited friends in France and Italy.__

7. who is pulling on my shirt? __Who is pulling on my shirt?__

8. the rocky mountains are very tall and beautiful. __The Rocky Mountains are very tall and beautiful.__

9. jeremy and i play clarinet in the band. __Jeremy and I play clarinet in the band.__

10. i would like to have a thick steak for dinner on my birthday. __I would like to have a thick steak for dinner on my birthday.__

11. isobel drank tea in london, england. __Isobel drank tea in London, England.__

12. last tuesday, john broke his leg. __Last Tuesday, John broke his leg.__

© Carson-Dellosa CD-3761   71

Name _____   Skill: Capitalization

Rule

Remember to use **capital letters** for:
  • the first word in a sentence • the pronoun "I"
  • proper nouns • important words in book and movie titles

Each sentence has one or more capitalization mistakes. Write each sentence correctly on the line below it.

1. my friend tony and i like chocolate ice cream. __My friend Tony and I like chocolate ice cream.__

2. after school today, paul and mike will have a race. __After school today, Paul and Mike will have a race.__

3. i go to brandford elementary school. __I go to Brandford Elementary School.__

4. how often does your mother take you to the mall? __How often does your mother take you to the mall?__

5. mr. davis is the best teacher in our school. __Mr. Davis is the best teacher in our school.__

6. myron's family just moved to lincoln, nebraska. __Myron's family just moved to Lincoln, Nebraska.__

7. jessie played in a concert last april. __Jessie played in a concert last April.__

8. i am reading a book called the mysterious stranger. __I am reading a book called The Mysterious Stranger.__

9. amy and beth are two characters in the book little women. __Amy and Beth are two characters in the book Little Women.__

10. the nile river flows through egypt. __The Nile River flows through Egypt.__

11. that mummy looks a lot like king tut! __That mummy looks a lot like King Tut!__

12. have you ever visited chicago? __Have you ever visited Chicago?__

© Carson-Dellosa CD-3761   72

Answer Key

Page 73

Name _____   Skill: Addition of Two Digits

Add.

#		#		#		#		#		#		#	
1.	97 +37 = **134**	2.	83 +58 = **141**	3.	68 +34 = **102**	4.	56 +92 = **148**	5.	69 +42 = **111**	6.	27 +58 = **85**	7.	91 +29 = **120**
8.	46 +57 = **103**	9.	65 +48 = **113**	10.	51 +79 = **130**	11.	78 +32 = **110**	12.	63 +78 = **141**	13.	49 +83 = **132**	14.	74 +78 = **152**
15.	27 +84 = **111**	16.	47 +76 = **123**	17.	42 +89 = **131**	18.	63 +51 = **114**	19.	74 +29 = **103**	20.	92 +76 = **168**	21.	59 +16 = **75**
22.	25 +57 = **82**	23.	57 +42 = **99**	24.	64 +57 = **121**	25.	86 +17 = **103**	26.	35 +28 = **63**	27.	54 +85 = **139**	28.	17 +66 = **83**
29.	56 +45 = **101**	30.	79 +24 = **103**	31.	39 +52 = **91**	32.	58 +43 = **101**	33.	73 +27 = **100**	34.	93 +45 = **138**	35.	87 +26 = **113**
36.	84 +26 = **110**	37.	37 +73 = **110**	38.	46 +49 = **95**	39.	63 +57 = **120**	40.	84 +34 = **118**	41.	79 +42 = **121**	42.	52 +57 = **109**
43.	45 +56 = **101**	44.	59 +33 = **92**	45.	49 +23 = **72**	46.	26 +68 = **94**	47.	65 +25 = **90**	48.	86 +48 = **134**	49.	36 +27 = **63**

73

Page 74

Name _____   Skill: Addition of Two Digits

Add.

#		#		#		#		#		#		#	
1.	43 +59 = **102**	2.	27 +55 = **82**	3.	86 +27 = **113**	4.	58 +46 = **104**	5.	25 +69 = **94**	6.	87 +44 = **131**	7.	87 +29 = **116**
8.	99 +29 = **128**	9.	53 +78 = **131**	10.	48 +67 = **115**	11.	75 +58 = **133**	12.	91 +39 = **130**	13.	33 +79 = **112**	14.	84 +87 = **171**
15.	69 +84 = **153**	16.	93 +88 = **181**	17.	72 +89 = **161**	18.	45 +78 = **123**	19.	64 +98 = **162**	20.	86 +36 = **122**	21.	26 +97 = **123**
22.	96 +58 = **154**	23.	56 +86 = **142**	24.	79 +38 = **117**	25.	86 +27 = **113**	26.	94 +47 = **141**	27.	36 +78 = **114**	28.	76 +45 = **121**
29.	89 +47 = **136**	30.	58 +62 = **120**	31.	73 +49 = **122**	32.	86 +76 = **162**	33.	78 +25 = **103**	34.	95 +61 = **156**	35.	57 +58 = **115**
36.	38 +87 = **125**	37.	64 +83 = **147**	38.	69 +52 = **121**	39.	77 +54 = **131**	40.	93 +58 = **151**	41.	65 +43 = **108**	42.	79 +79 = **158**
43.	56 +77 = **133**	44.	77 +64 = **141**	45.	85 +68 = **153**	46.	27 +87 = **114**	47.	89 +23 = **112**	48.	58 +44 = **102**	49.	93 +28 = **121**

74

Page 75

Name _____   Skill: Addition of Three Digits

Add.

#		#		#		#		#		#		#	
1.	358 +227 = **585**	2.	371 +389 = **760**	3.	408 +159 = **567**	4.	327 +196 = **523**	5.	417 +125 = **542**	6.	730 +197 = **927**	7.	344 +523 = **867**
8.	751 +225 = **976**	9.	400 +127 = **527**	10.	111 +345 = **456**	11.	250 +178 = **428**	12.	219 +470 = **689**	13.	382 +160 = **542**	14.	348 +436 = **784**
15.	709 +189 = **898**	16.	522 +157 = **679**	17.	398 +145 = **543**	18.	270 +134 = **404**	19.	520 +177 = **697**	20.	254 +384 = **638**	21.	331 +245 = **576**
22.	428 +150 = **578**	23.	197 +402 = **599**	24.	724 +150 = **874**	25.	181 +199 = **380**	26.	533 +238 = **771**	27.	451 +315 = **766**	28.	613 +178 = **791**
29.	357 +417 = **774**	30.	519 +170 = **689**	31.	834 +196 = **1,030**	32.	313 +488 = **801**	33.	558 +184 = **742**	34.	687 +139 = **826**	35.	901 +149 = **1,050**
36.	410 +291 = **701**	37.	737 +288 = **1,025**	38.	426 +497 = **923**	39.	166 +617 = **783**	40.	404 +395 = **799**	41.	259 +450 = **709**	42.	272 +438 = **710**
43.	106 +329 = **435**	44.	857 +341 = **1,198**	45.	849 +254 = **1,103**	46.	426 +208 = **634**	47.	572 +259 = **831**	48.	553 +347 = **900**	49.	295 +486 = **781**

75

Page 76

Name _____   Skill: Subtraction of One and Two Digits

Subtract.

#		#		#		#		#		#		#	
1.	3 −2 = **1**	2.	7 −0 = **7**	3.	9 −4 = **5**	4.	7 −3 = **4**	5.	8 −8 = **0**	6.	5 −2 = **3**	7.	9 −4 = **5**
8.	4 −2 = **2**	9.	9 −7 = **2**	10.	10 −4 = **6**	11.	6 −1 = **5**	12.	9 −8 = **1**	13.	2 −1 = **1**	14.	8 −3 = **5**
15.	10 −9 = **1**	16.	12 −5 = **7**	17.	11 −4 = **7**	18.	10 −7 = **3**	19.	2 −2 = **0**	20.	15 −6 = **9**	21.	13 −8 = **5**
22.	8 −4 = **4**	23.	7 −2 = **5**	24.	14 −5 = **9**	25.	11 −9 = **2**	26.	17 −9 = **8**	27.	5 −3 = **2**	28.	13 −6 = **7**
29.	14 −6 = **8**	30.	9 −9 = **0**	31.	14 −7 = **7**	32.	13 −9 = **4**	33.	8 −2 = **6**	34.	12 −9 = **3**	35.	16 −7 = **9**
36.	10 −2 = **8**	37.	18 −9 = **9**	38.	12 −5 = **7**	39.	16 −7 = **9**	40.	14 −5 = **9**	41.	9 −7 = **2**	42.	17 −8 = **9**
43.	10 −6 = **4**	44.	7 −6 = **1**	45.	9 −6 = **3**	46.	6 −2 = **4**	47.	15 −8 = **7**	48.	15 −6 = **9**	49.	16 −8 = **8**

76

117

Answer Key

Name _____ Skill: Subtraction of Two Digits

Subtract.

1. 30 − 10 = 20
2. 70 − 40 = 30
3. 90 − 40 = 50
4. 60 − 30 = 30
5. 80 − 80 = 0
6. 50 − 20 = 30
7. 90 − 10 = 80
8. 40 − 20 = 20
9. 90 − 70 = 20
10. 50 − 40 = 10
11. 60 − 10 = 50
12. 90 − 80 = 10
13. 20 − 10 = 10
14. 80 − 30 = 50
15. 55 − 43 = 12
16. 72 − 50 = 22
17. 88 − 41 = 47
18. 33 − 22 = 11
19. 72 − 32 = 40
20. 75 − 64 = 11
21. 99 − 48 = 51
22. 87 − 46 = 41
23. 78 − 24 = 54
24. 83 − 51 = 32
25. 69 − 19 = 50
26. 76 − 45 = 31
27. 58 − 30 = 28
28. 66 − 62 = 4
29. 72 − 61 = 11
30. 98 − 46 = 52
31. 33 − 12 = 21
32. 84 − 23 = 61
33. 88 − 72 = 16
34. 48 − 32 = 16
35. 76 − 51 = 25
36. 95 − 23 = 72
37. 80 − 40 = 40
38. 67 − 51 = 16
39. 82 − 70 = 12
40. 96 − 53 = 43
41. 79 − 17 = 62
42. 87 − 47 = 40
43. 80 − 60 = 20
44. 70 − 60 = 10
45. 93 − 60 = 33
46. 57 − 23 = 34
47. 77 − 17 = 60
48. 84 − 62 = 22
49. 93 − 71 = 22

77

Name _____ Skill: Subtraction of Two Digits

Subtract.

1. 91 − 56 = 35
2. 52 − 49 = 3
3. 43 − 38 = 5
4. 71 − 34 = 37
5. 75 − 46 = 29
6. 84 − 47 = 37
7. 61 − 12 = 49
8. 86 − 58 = 28
9. 90 − 29 = 61
10. 42 − 28 = 14
11. 94 − 66 = 28
12. 62 − 49 = 13
13. 55 − 17 = 38
14. 41 − 25 = 16
15. 86 − 39 = 47
16. 34 − 18 = 16
17. 73 − 38 = 35
18. 44 − 15 = 29
19. 73 − 25 = 48
20. 58 − 39 = 19
21. 52 − 24 = 28
22. 38 − 19 = 19
23. 46 − 28 = 18
24. 53 − 28 = 25
25. 95 − 48 = 47
26. 84 − 27 = 57
27. 64 − 39 = 25
28. 92 − 59 = 33
29. 87 − 38 = 49
30. 74 − 25 = 49
31. 67 − 38 = 29
32. 71 − 64 = 7
33. 83 − 28 = 55
34. 41 − 34 = 7
35. 71 − 42 = 29
36. 93 − 75 = 18
37. 84 − 19 = 65
38. 82 − 73 = 9
39. 84 − 37 = 47
40. 66 − 48 = 18
41. 75 − 27 = 48
42. 54 − 39 = 15
43. 75 − 17 = 58
44. 47 − 18 = 29
45. 40 − 29 = 11
46. 61 − 23 = 38
47. 54 − 38 = 16
48. 81 − 27 = 54
49. 67 − 38 = 29

78

Name _____ Skill: Subtraction of Three Digits

Subtract.

1. 326 − 285 = 41
2. 972 − 609 = 363
3. 685 − 246 = 439
4. 518 − 329 = 189
5. 741 − 362 = 379
6. 438 − 258 = 180
7. 371 − 283 = 88
8. 529 − 482 = 47
9. 625 − 407 = 218
10. 514 − 126 = 388
11. 664 − 278 = 386
12. 742 − 467 = 275
13. 200 − 158 = 42
14. 634 − 277 = 357
15. 423 − 285 = 138
16. 222 − 153 = 69
17. 435 − 166 = 269
18. 628 − 499 = 129
19. 757 − 178 = 579
20. 637 − 388 = 249
21. 423 − 285 = 138
22. 533 − 240 = 293
23. 415 − 196 = 219
24. 382 − 175 = 207
25. 632 − 377 = 255
26. 585 − 423 = 162
27. 778 − 439 = 339
28. 130 − 115 = 15
29. 623 − 194 = 429
30. 900 − 309 = 591
31. 722 − 317 = 405
32. 377 − 186 = 191
33. 871 − 384 = 487
34. 628 − 300 = 328
35. 454 − 279 = 175
36. 990 − 731 = 259
37. 818 − 693 = 125
38. 572 − 335 = 237
39. 951 − 357 = 594
40. 825 − 469 = 356
41. 771 − 217 = 554
42. 943 − 761 = 182
43. 407 − 328 = 79
44. 431 − 298 = 133
45. 906 − 682 = 224
46. 486 − 297 = 189
47. 615 − 288 = 327
48. 883 − 227 = 656
49. 631 − 156 = 475

79

Name _____ Skill: Multiplication Facts through Ten

Multiply.

1. 3 × 2 = 6
2. 7 × 0 = 0
3. 9 × 3 = 27
4. 3 × 1 = 3
5. 8 × 2 = 16
6. 5 × 2 = 10
7. 3 × 7 = 21
8. 1 × 2 = 2
9. 0 × 8 = 0
10. 3 × 4 = 12
11. 2 × 9 = 18
12. 9 × 0 = 0
13. 2 × 1 = 2
14. 8 × 3 = 24
15. 9 × 1 = 9
16. 6 × 3 = 18
17. 0 × 4 = 0
18. 5 × 1 = 5
19. 2 × 2 = 4
20. 5 × 3 = 15
21. 3 × 2 = 6
22. 8 × 0 = 0
23. 8 × 3 = 24
24. 1 × 5 = 5
25. 3 × 9 = 27
26. 9 × 2 = 18
27. 5 × 0 = 0
28. 3 × 6 = 18
29. 6 × 0 = 0
30. 9 × 3 = 27
31. 1 × 7 = 7
32. 3 × 3 = 9
33. 8 × 2 = 16
34. 2 × 1 = 2
35. 7 × 2 = 14
36. 10 × 2 = 20
37. 0 × 9 = 0
38. 2 × 0 = 0
39. 3 × 5 = 15
40. 0 × 1 = 0
41. 3 × 9 = 27
42. 8 × 2 = 16
43. 6 × 3 = 18
44. 7 × 1 = 7
45. 2 × 6 = 12
46. 4 × 2 = 8
47. 5 × 0 = 0
48. 1 × 4 = 4
49. 10 × 6 = 60

80

Answer Key

Name _____ Skill: Multiplication Facts through Eleven

Multiply.

1.	2.	3.	4.	5.	6.	7.
10	7	6	3	8	11	3
x 4	x 5	x 3	x 7	x 5	x 2	x 6
40	**35**	**18**	**21**	**40**	**22**	**18**

8.	9.	10.	11.	12.	13.	14.
1	0	6	10	9	5	8
x 4	x 5	x 4	x 9	x 4	x 1	x 6
4	**0**	**24**	**90**	**36**	**5**	**48**

15.	16.	17.	18.	19.	20.	21.
9	11	0	5	4	5	3
x 4	x 5	x 6	x 7	x 2	x 5	x 6
36	**55**	**0**	**35**	**8**	**25**	**18**

22.	23.	24.	25.	26.	27.	28.
11	8	1	6	9	5	6
x 7	x 4	x 5	x 9	x 7	x 4	x 6
77	**32**	**5**	**54**	**63**	**20**	**36**

29.	30.	31.	32.	33.	34.	35.
6	9	4	3	10	2	7
x 6	x 5	x 7	x 7	x 5	x 4	x 7
36	**45**	**28**	**21**	**50**	**8**	**49**

36.	37.	38.	39.	40.	41.	42.
10	4	5	8	6	11	7
x 4	x 1	x 0	x 5	x 1	x 6	x 9
40	**4**	**5**	**40**	**6**	**66**	**63**

43.	44.	45.	46.	47.	48.	49.
6	7	7	10	5	7	11
x 7	x 7	x 6	x 2	x 6	x 4	x 3
42	**49**	**42**	**20**	**30**	**28**	**33**

81

Name _____ Skill: Multiplication Facts through Twelve

Multiply.

1.	2.	3.	4.	5.	6.	7.
8	7	10	11	8	9	10
x 3	x 9	x 3	x 3	x 8	x 2	x 7
24	**63**	**30**	**33**	**64**	**18**	**70**

8.	9.	10.	11.	12.	13.	14.
12	10	9	8	10	12	8
x 2	x 8	x 4	x 9	x 9	x 1	x 3
24	**80**	**36**	**72**	**90**	**12**	**24**

15.	16.	17.	18.	19.	20.	21.
12	6	10	12	10	8	9
x 9	x 9	x 4	x 5	x 2	x 3	x 8
108	**54**	**40**	**60**	**20**	**24**	**72**

22.	23.	24.	25.	26.	27.	28.
11	8	12	7	9	10	11
x 0	x 3	x 5	x 8	x 9	x 3	x 6
0	**24**	**60**	**56**	**81**	**30**	**66**

29.	30.	31.	32.	33.	34.	35.
10	9	11	3	8	10	7
x 6	x 3	x 7	x 8	x 8	x 2	x 9
60	**27**	**77**	**24**	**64**	**20**	**56**

36.	37.	38.	39.	40.	41.	42.
11	10	2	8	10	11	10
x 2	x 9	x 9	x 5	x 1	x 9	x 7
22	**90**	**18**	**40**	**10**	**99**	**70**

43.	44.	45.	46.	47.	48.	49.
11	7	10	12	5	9	12
x 6	x 8	x 6	x 6	x 9	x 4	x 6
66	**56**	**60**	**72**	**45**	**36**	**72**

82

Name _____ Skill: One-Digit Divisors

Divide.

1.	2.	3.	4.	5.
9	**3**	**8**	**4**	**4**
2⟌18	3⟌9	3⟌24	1⟌4	2⟌8

6.	7.	8.	9.	10.
5	**8**	**12**	**1**	**10**
3⟌15	4⟌32	1⟌12	3⟌3	2⟌20

11.	12.	13.	14.	15.
4	**12**	**2**	**11**	**1**
4⟌16	3⟌36	1⟌2	4⟌44	2⟌2

16.	17.	18.	19.	20.
8	**3**	**7**	**3**	**9**
1⟌8	2⟌6	3⟌21	4⟌12	3⟌27

21.	22.	23.	24.	25.
2	**10**	**12**	**2**	**10**
4⟌8	1⟌10	2⟌24	2⟌4	3⟌30

26.	27.	28.	29.	30.
12	**11**	**6**	**7**	**5**
4⟌48	3⟌33	4⟌24	2⟌14	4⟌20

83

Name _____ Skill: One-Digit Divisors

Divide.

1.	2.	3.	4.	5.
3	**7**	**1**	**2**	**12**
5⟌15	6⟌42	7⟌7	6⟌12	8⟌96

6.	7.	8.	9.	10.
6	**5**	**8**	**3**	**10**
5⟌30	7⟌35	5⟌40	8⟌24	6⟌60

11.	12.	13.	14.	15.
3	**9**	**1**	**9**	**6**
6⟌18	7⟌63	5⟌5	8⟌72	6⟌36

16.	17.	18.	19.	20.
10	**12**	**4**	**11**	**2**
8⟌80	5⟌60	7⟌28	6⟌66	7⟌14

21.	22.	23.	24.	25.
7	**1**	**6**	**10**	**11**
5⟌35	6⟌6	8⟌48	5⟌50	8⟌88

26.	27.	28.	29.	30.
4	**9**	**11**	**8**	**8**
8⟌32	5⟌45	7⟌77	8⟌64	6⟌48

84

Answer Key

Name _____ Skill: One- and Two-Digit Divisors

Divide.

1. $\frac{10}{9\overline{)90}}$ 2. $\frac{2}{10\overline{)20}}$ 3. $\frac{9}{11\overline{)99}}$ 4. $\frac{9}{12\overline{)108}}$ 5. $\frac{7}{11\overline{)77}}$

6. $\frac{2}{12\overline{)24}}$ 7. $\frac{6}{10\overline{)60}}$ 8. $\frac{5}{12\overline{)60}}$ 9. $\frac{10}{11\overline{)110}}$ 10. $\frac{10}{10\overline{)100}}$

11. $\frac{3}{9\overline{)27}}$ 12. $\frac{1}{9\overline{)9}}$ 13. $\frac{12}{10\overline{)120}}$ 14. $\frac{11}{11\overline{)121}}$ 15. $\frac{12}{9\overline{)108}}$

16. $\frac{8}{1\overline{)8}}$ 17. $\frac{3}{2\overline{)6}}$ 18. $\frac{7}{3\overline{)21}}$ 19. $\frac{3}{4\overline{)12}}$ 20. $\frac{9}{3\overline{)27}}$

21. $\frac{4}{9\overline{)36}}$ 22. $\frac{4}{10\overline{)40}}$ 23. $\frac{3}{12\overline{)36}}$ 24. $\frac{12}{11\overline{)132}}$ 25. $\frac{4}{9\overline{)36}}$

26. $\frac{5}{9\overline{)45}}$ 27. $\frac{4}{11\overline{)44}}$ 28. $\frac{12}{12\overline{)144}}$ 29. $\frac{11}{10\overline{)110}}$ 30. $\frac{11}{11\overline{)121}}$

© Carson-Dellosa CD-3761   85

Name _____ Skill: Place Value

Use the given number to find the place values. The first one has been done for you.

1. The number is: **7,320,194.685**

   a. Name the digit in the tens place. _____ 9
   b. Name the digit in the tenths place. _____ 6
   c. Name the digit in the millions place. _____ 7
   d. Name the digit in the ones place. _____ 4
   e. In what place value is the digit "0"? _____ thousands
   f. In what place value is the digit "4"? _____ ones
   g. In what place value is the digit "3"? _____ hundred thousands
   h. In what place value is the digit "5"? _____ thousandths

2. The number is: **8,635.147**

   a. Name the digit in the hundreds place. _____ 6
   b. Name the digit in the hundredths place. _____ 4
   c. Name the digit in the thousands place. _____ 8
   d. Name the digit in the tenths place. _____ 1
   e. Name the number that is one hundred more. _____ 8,735.147
   f. Name the number that is one thousand less. _____ 7,635.147
   g. Name the number that is one-hundredth less. _____ 8,635.137
   h. Name the number that is one more. _____ 8,636.147

3. The number is: **1,320,796.485**

   a. Name the digit in the millions place. _____ 1
   b. Name the digit in the ones place. _____ 6
   c. Name the digit in the thousandths place. _____ 5
   d. Name the digit in the ten thousands place. _____ 2
   e. Name the number that is ten thousand less. _____ 1,310,796.485
   f. Name the number that is one-thousandth more. _____ 1,320,796.486
   g. Name the number that is one less. _____ 1,320,795.485
   h. Name the number that is one million more. _____ 2,320,796.485

© Carson-Dellosa CD-3761   86

Name _____ Skill: Place Value

Use the given number to find the place values. The first one has been done for you.

1. The number is: **453,621.908**

   a. Name the digit in the thousands place. _____ 3
   b. Name the digit in the hundredths place. _____ 0
   c. Name the digit in the ten thousands place. _____ 5
   d. Name the digit in the ones place. _____ 1
   e. In what place value is the digit "8"? _____ thousandths
   f. In what place value is the digit "4"? _____ hundred thousands
   g. In what place value is the digit "9"? _____ tenths
   h. In what place value is the digit "5"? _____ ten thousands

2. The number is: **45,923.0168**

   a. Name the digit in the hundreds place. _____ 9
   b. Name the digit in the hundredths place. _____ 1
   c. Name the digit in the thousands place. _____ 5
   d. Name the digit in the thousandths place. _____ 6
   e. Name the number that is ten more. _____ 45,933.0168
   f. Name the number that is one thousand less. _____ 44,923.0168
   g. Name the number that is one-hundredth less. _____ 45,923.0068
   h. Name the number that is one more. _____ 45,924.0168

3. The number is: **5,023,178.496**

   a. Name the digit in the millions place. _____ 5
   b. Name the digit in the ones place. _____ 8
   c. Name the digit in the hundredths place. _____ 9
   d. Name the digit in the hundred thousands place. _____ 0
   e. Name the number that is ten thousand less. _____ 5,013,178.496
   f. Name the number that is one-thousandth more. _____ 5,023,178.497
   g. Name the number that is one less. _____ 5,023,177.496
   h. Name the number that is one million more. _____ 6,023,178.496

© Carson-Dellosa CD-3761   87

Name _____ Skill: Rounding

1. Round these numbers to the nearest ten. The first one has been done for you.

   a. 23 _____ 20   f. 48 _____ 50
   b. 59 _____ 60   g. 96 _____ 100
   c. 237 _____ 240   h. 151 _____ 150
   d. 468 _____ 470   i. 375 _____ 380
   e. 783 _____ 780   j. 994 _____ 990

2. Round these numbers to the nearest hundred. The first one has been done for you.

   a. 749 _____ 700   k. 637 _____ 600
   b. 291 _____ 300   l. 590 _____ 600
   c. 453 _____ 500   m. 849 _____ 800
   d. 1,658 _____ 1,700 n. 5,267 _____ 5,300
   e. 3,409 _____ 3,400 o. 3,721 _____ 3,700
   f. 872 _____ 900   p. 75 _____ 100
   g. 7,433 _____ 7,400 q. 382 _____ 400
   h. 6,551 _____ 6,600 r. 5,098 _____ 5,100
   i. 3,929 _____ 3,900 s. 4,629 _____ 4,600
   j. 8,494 _____ 8,500 t. 9,712 _____ 9,700

3. Round these numbers to the nearest thousand. The first one has been done for you.

   a. 2,282 _____ 2,000   f. 4,503 _____ 5,000
   b. 5,499 _____ 5,000   g. 8,457 _____ 8,000
   c. 7,911 _____ 8,000   h. 6,386 _____ 6,000
   d. 17,695 _____ 18,000 i. 14,623 _____ 15,000
   e. 20,392 _____ 20,000 j. 19,821 _____ 20,000

© Carson-Dellosa CD-3761   88

Answer Key

Answer Key

Name _____ Skill: Fraction Subtraction

Subtract. Write each answer in simplest form. The first one has been done for you.

1. $\frac{12}{13} - \frac{11}{13} = \boxed{\frac{1}{13}}$ 2. $\frac{5}{5} - \frac{2}{5} = \boxed{\frac{3}{5}}$

3. $\frac{7}{7} - \frac{4}{7} = \boxed{\frac{3}{7}}$ 4. $\frac{8}{9} - \frac{4}{9} = \boxed{\frac{4}{9}}$

5. $\frac{6}{8} - \frac{3}{8} = \boxed{\frac{3}{8}}$ 6. $\frac{3}{4} - \frac{2}{4} = \boxed{\frac{1}{4}}$

7. $\frac{8}{9} - \frac{1}{9} = \boxed{\frac{7}{9}}$ 8. $\frac{6}{6} - \frac{5}{6} = \boxed{\frac{1}{6}}$

9. $\frac{5}{7} - \frac{2}{7} = \boxed{\frac{3}{7}}$ 10. $\frac{4}{7} - \frac{2}{7} = \boxed{\frac{2}{7}}$

11. $\frac{8}{9} - \frac{7}{9} = \boxed{\frac{1}{9}}$ 12. $\frac{5}{6} - \frac{2}{6} = \boxed{\frac{1}{2}}$

13. $\frac{2}{6} - \frac{1}{6} = \boxed{\frac{1}{6}}$ 14. $\frac{5}{7} - \frac{1}{7} = \boxed{\frac{4}{7}}$

15. $\frac{3}{4} - \frac{1}{4} = \boxed{\frac{1}{2}}$ 16. $\frac{7}{8} - \frac{3}{8} = \boxed{\frac{1}{2}}$

© Carson-Dellosa CD-3761   93

Name _____ Skill: Less than, Greater than, Equal to

Compare the fractions. Write <, >, or = in each square to make a true math statement. The first one has been done for you.

1. $\frac{1}{2}$ $\boxed{=}$ $\frac{6}{12}$ 2. $\frac{3}{4}$ $\boxed{>}$ $\frac{1}{4}$

3. $\frac{1}{4}$ $\boxed{<}$ $\frac{5}{10}$ 4. $\frac{1}{3}$ $\boxed{<}$ $\frac{5}{6}$

5. $\frac{2}{3}$ $\boxed{<}$ $\frac{5}{6}$ 6. $\frac{4}{8}$ $\boxed{>}$ $\frac{1}{3}$

7. $\frac{4}{5}$ $\boxed{>}$ $\frac{7}{10}$ 8. $\frac{4}{9}$ $\boxed{<}$ $\frac{1}{2}$

9. $\frac{3}{9}$ $\boxed{=}$ $\frac{1}{3}$ 10. $\frac{5}{6}$ $\boxed{>}$ $\frac{2}{3}$

11. $\frac{2}{8}$ $\boxed{<}$ $\frac{2}{3}$ 12. $\frac{5}{7}$ $\boxed{<}$ $\frac{7}{8}$

13. $\frac{4}{5}$ $\boxed{>}$ $\frac{3}{4}$ 14. $\frac{1}{9}$ $\boxed{<}$ $\frac{1}{5}$

15. $\frac{1}{6}$ $\boxed{=}$ $\frac{2}{12}$ 16. $\frac{2}{8}$ $\boxed{=}$ $\frac{1}{4}$

© Carson-Dellosa CD-3761   94

Name _____ Skill: Less than, Greater than, Equal to

Compare the fractions. Write <, >, or = in each square to make a true math statement. The first one has been done for you.

1. $\frac{1}{6}$ $\boxed{<}$ $\frac{1}{4}$ 2. $\frac{3}{5}$ $\boxed{>}$ $\frac{1}{3}$

3. $\frac{3}{4}$ $\boxed{>}$ $\frac{1}{2}$ 4. $\frac{1}{2}$ $\boxed{=}$ $\frac{6}{12}$

5. $\frac{4}{5}$ $\boxed{>}$ $\frac{3}{10}$ 6. $\frac{5}{9}$ $\boxed{>}$ $\frac{1}{3}$

7. $\frac{6}{9}$ $\boxed{=}$ $\frac{2}{3}$ 8. $\frac{4}{5}$ $\boxed{>}$ $\frac{3}{4}$

9. $\frac{1}{4}$ $\boxed{>}$ $\frac{1}{7}$ 10. $\frac{2}{4}$ $\boxed{=}$ $\frac{1}{2}$

11. $\frac{2}{3}$ $\boxed{<}$ $\frac{5}{6}$ 12. $\frac{1}{6}$ $\boxed{<}$ $\frac{1}{3}$

13. $\frac{2}{9}$ $\boxed{<}$ $\frac{3}{4}$ 14. $\frac{5}{7}$ $\boxed{>}$ $\frac{3}{8}$

15. $\frac{4}{6}$ $\boxed{>}$ $\frac{1}{2}$ 16. $\frac{6}{8}$ $\boxed{=}$ $\frac{3}{4}$

© Carson-Dellosa CD-3761   95

Name _____ Skill: Word Problems

Read the paragraph carefully, then answer the questions. Write **NG** if there is not enough information given to answer the question.

Trenice sells insurance over the telephone. She makes many calls but does not always make a sale. This week she did pretty well! Monday she made 112 calls and 23 sales. Tuesday she made 94 calls and 31 sales. Wednesday Trenice made 67 calls and only 14 sales. She made 100 calls and 12 sales on Thursday. Friday was Trenice's day off so she went to the beach!

1. **How many calls did Trenice make on Wednesday and Friday?**
   She made 67 phone calls.

2. **How many sales did Trenice make this week?**
   She made 80 sales this week.

3. **How many calls did she make in all this week?**
   She made 373 calls this week.

4. **How many more calls did Trenice make than sales?**
   She made 293 more calls than sales.

5. **What did Trenice do on Saturday?**
   NG

6. **How many sales were made on Tuesday, Wednesday, and Thursday?**
   She made 57 sales.

7. **On Tuesday, how many more calls than sales were made?**
   63 more calls than sales were made on Tuesday.

8. **How many more calls were made on Monday than on Thursday?**
   Twelve more calls were made on Monday.

© Carson-Dellosa CD-3761   96

Answer Key

Name _____   Skill: Word Problems

Read the paragraph carefully, then answer the questions. Write **NG** if there is not enough information given to answer the question.

David, Bobby, and Sam play on the Eagles baseball team. This season Bobby hit 9 home runs and 14 singles. David hit 10 home runs and 18 singles. Sam hit 3 home runs and 24 singles. The Eagles won 22 games and lost 8 games this season.

1. **What is the name of the boys' team?**
   The boys' team is called the Eagles.

2. **What sport do the boys play?**
   They play baseball.

3. **How many home runs did all three boys hit this season?**
   They hit 22 home runs.

4. **Which boy hit the most singles?**
   Sam hit the most singles.

5. **How many games did the team play this season?**
   The Eagles played 30 games.

6. **How many more singles than home runs did Sam hit?**
   Sam hit 21 more singles.

7. **How many singles did David and Bobby hit this season?**
   They hit 32 singles.

8. **Which boy hit the least number of home runs?**
   Sam hit the least number of home runs (3).

© Carson-Dellosa CD-3761   97

Name _____   Skill: Word Problems

Read the paragraph and chart carefully, then answer the questions. Write **NG** if there is not enough information given to answer the question.

Kasey kept track of the rainfall for her state for five months. Her findings are listed on the chart at the right.

April	14 inches
May	9 inches
June	8 inches
July	9 inches
August	12 inches

1. **How many months did Kasey keep a record of the rainfall?**
   She kept a record for 5 months.

2. **In which state does Kasey live?**
   NG

3. **How much more rain fell in April than in August?**
   Two more inches fell in April.

4. **Which two months had the same amount of rainfall?**
   May and July each had 9 inches.

5. **How much rain fell in April, May, and June?**
   Thirty-one inches of rain fell in April, May, and June.

6. **What was the total amount of rainfall for all five months?**
   The total was 52 inches.

7. **Which month had the lowest amount of rainfall?**
   June had the least rainfall.

8. **What was the difference in rainfall between April and June?**
   The difference was six inches.

© Carson-Dellosa CD-3761   98

$2\overline{)10}$ $2\overline{)18}$ $3\overline{)12}$ $3\overline{)24}$

$2\overline{)8}$ $2\overline{)16}$ $3\overline{)9}$ $3\overline{)21}$

$2\overline{)6}$ $2\overline{)14}$ $3\overline{)6}$ $3\overline{)18}$

$2\overline{)4}$ $2\overline{)12}$ $3\overline{)3}$ $3\overline{)15}$

5

9

4

8

7

3

8

4

6

2

7

3

5

1

6

2

$6\overline{)6}$ $6\overline{)30}$ $7\overline{)7}$ $7\overline{)35}$

$5\overline{)45}$ $6\overline{)24}$ $6\overline{)54}$ $7\overline{)28}$

$5\overline{)40}$ $6\overline{)18}$ $6\overline{)48}$ $7\overline{)21}$

$5\overline{)35}$ $6\overline{)12}$ $6\overline{)42}$ $7\overline{)14}$

1

5

1

5

9

4

6

4

8

3

8

3

7

2

7

2

2 x 9	3 x 3	3 x 4	3 x 5
© CD-3761	© CD-3761	© CD-3761	© CD-3761
3 x 6	3 x 7	3 x 8	3 x 9
© CD-3761	© CD-3761	© CD-3761	© CD-3761
4 x 4	4 x 5	4 x 6	4 x 7
© CD-3761	© CD-3761	© CD-3761	© CD-3761
4 x 8	4 x 9	5 x 5	5 x 6
© CD-3761	© CD-3761	© CD-3761	© CD-3761

15	**12**	**9**	**18**
© CD-3761	© CD-3761	© CD-3761	© CD-3761
27	**24**	**21**	**18**
© CD-3761	© CD-3761	© CD-3761	© CD-3761
28	**24**	**20**	**16**
© CD-3761	© CD-3761	© CD-3761	© CD-3761
30	**25**	**36**	**32**
© CD-3761	© CD-3761	© CD-3761	© CD-3761

affection

© CD-3761

connect

© CD-3761

convince

© CD-3761

exhibit

© CD-3761

adverb

© CD-3761

climate

© CD-3761

contraction

© CD-3761

educate

© CD-3761

adopt

© CD-3761

brittle

© CD-3761

context

© CD-3761

doze

© CD-3761

adjective

© CD-3761

antonym

© CD-3761

contact

© CD-3761

disguise

© CD-3761

homophone	hesitate	gesture	extend
© CD-3761	© CD-3761	© CD-3761	© CD-3761
massive	loyal	locate	humble
© CD-3761	© CD-3761	© CD-3761	© CD-3761
predicate	pollute	observer	noun
© CD-3761	© CD-3761	© CD-3761	© CD-3761
recover	pursuit	pronoun	progress
© CD-3761	© CD-3761	© CD-3761	© CD-3761

request

© CD-3761

snare

© CD-3761

tingle

© CD-3761

wobble

© CD-3761

remainder

© CD-3761

sloppy

© CD-3761

synonym

© CD-3761

weary

© CD-3761

relative

© CD-3761

seize

© CD-3761

suggestion

© CD-3761

vocabulary

© CD-3761

region

© CD-3761

respond

© CD-3761

subject

© CD-3761

verb

© CD-3761

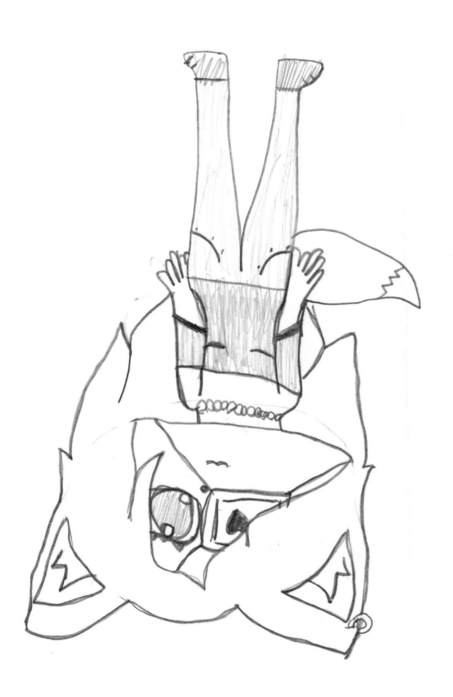